The 21st Century Poetry Revolution

by Albert Nyangaresi

country kenya
year of publishing 2024

1.Soon

"Soon"
Soon am coming dear
Soon just like now
Am coming my love
My sunshine am coming
I feel to test soup
Time has gone tiii
Now my moonlight
I feel to be fed by hands
Of mi Amor
Soon is hear
Long awaited from anos
To months to weeks
Weeks to days to date
Seeing mi la novia
What awesome seen
Seeing mi spend thrift
Soon am home home
Mi Amor soon am there
Soon not far from hoy
It's soon when l gonna
Disfruta with mi amor
When l gonna see padres
Award them with regalo
When l gonna take mi
Baby girl to see sacred
Places particularly
Where l have invited
Mi dinero o pesos
Soon l gonna arrive

When we gonna
Share the left stories
Tiii date l have dated
No one just only you
Mi favorito one joan
Soon am coming
Soon gonna mark
The climax of wait
Soon am coming
Am there
Composed by Tibez Albershile

2. Away

"Away"
Away l got love
Away l got Skylark
Away learnt love
Away for first
I felt feelings
What l say away
Made me to love
Away l lost best
Friend for love
What to say
What is mistry
That es hidden
Indeed away
I learnt love
Isn't just love
Love is loyal
Away l see
Value de love
Not love just
For laugh
What away made
Tibez was indeed
Awesome only
From away l fed
Myself with virtues
For sure away made
Me a person not a joker
Away l erase eternity
Game of Bublé gam

Step by step
I away has given me
Bland be it decades
To be known by generations

Composed by Tibez Albershile

3.fear

"Fear"
Am fearing mi love
Your touching words
Your sweet sounds
You purely heart for
Me one day to change
Am in complex state
My amor my love es
A firm farmative
At state what about
Tomorrow
You are indeed
Queen to my heart
Queen of queen's
You have captured
My kingdom at your
Hands yet fearing
Mi Amor sweet of
Love led to blind
My eyes may fail
To see when you
Are with me my bird
That l fear
You my flew away
Yet l see you a regalo
That meant for me
Many in shape of sun
Have come mi darling
Yet you are one
Have choose on every

Life and breath of mine
Fear chake me but
I see your eyes pure
Fear l have its erased
Fear for you gonna go
It's not anymore your
Love joan just as a bc
Has completed me
What to say where it started
Only my Skylark can see
It and tell to universe
About our love
Love of fear de losing
Each other what love
True love test it you
Know it's key of life
Composed by Albert Nyangaresi

4.The mujer l married

"The Mujer l married"
Whom did l marry,
Am a dormant volcano,
What is essence and value,
De marriage am mad now,
Call me mad due to love,
Whom did l marry,
My migos mention ili,
About her yet was ignorant,
I saw love yet l failed to see,
Am blinded by love ,
What dilemma am l in ,
Facing one whom doesn't want,
My parents in this state,
Am a jew on summer season,
When did and how l made,
Such mistake in my life,
Whom did l marry,
I saw Skylark so unfortunate ,
To find l have invited devil,
Day in out it's fight no peace,
Surely l married a man ,
My house l can't even sit,
For a second before Satan,
Arrives with his dramas,
Whom did l marry,
Send me away if you can,
Tell me you wanna peace,
No peace no peace,
You can't do what you want,

I say not you in the house,
There will be no peace ,
Hopefully you get me clear,
Prepare supper so l can,
Be Full and sang for me,
A song before you begin ,
Preparing supper
Whom did l marry.
Composed by Map poetic editor

5.Goodbye

"Goodbye"
Mi stars indicated
That she gonna flew
Away yet my mind
Didn't allow l saw
Paradise only
Action speak more
Than words yet
I was stubborn now
Heed l payed to
Today it's farewell
Am a jew
To whom gonna
Love me more
Than her the one
True love isn't there
The pain of losing
A lover is hurting
Me deep down heart
What a day where
To hide the face
From facing reality
Adiós adiós
I can't love you
More than this
No more even friendship
We gonna have con
You since once
Below the line
We loved each other

Why why me
When l see l have
Found heart it's
Adiós farewell
Only preguntas
Mi Favourito Padre
Mi giver why all
I alone no more
Skylark even sunshine
The one whom impressed
Me mucho from
First day to date
Yet date is last day
To see mi Amor
Composed by Tibez Albershile

6. Awaited War

"Long awaited war"
We have waited
Enough de war our
Supply are diminishing
Our soldiers are growing
Weak and aged
The trees are shedding
Summer sunshine
Is finishing everything
Yet still waiting for war
The war has been fought
Decades tii date waiting
For same war that spread
The blood of our beloved
Ones war that even the
Cause of war we can't
Tell yet ready to fight
What a tragedy what
To say what to do war
War war everyone is war
Months has passed
Since last war was
Fought people's desires
For the war are now
Glowing weak like war
That we have been waiting
Isn't anymore now its peace
What peace can't believe
Peace no peace
All the blood shed go in vain

No no no
Soon signs are appearing
The matching of military
The trumpet of war is blown
Composed by Albert Nyangaresi

7. Save Me

"SAVE ME"
I really don't see tomorrow,
The dark doom is coming,
For me the past memories ,
Are chasing my heart l ,
Wonder what l wiii do,
The people l murdered,
The wealth l had snatch ,
People now curses are ,
Following me What to do,
Whom to call to save me,
The society everyone evade,
Me they see me monitor,
Who to save me my sins ,
I have committed can ,
Not allow me to sleep ,
At peace l have power ,
Everything to make me ,
Feel more powerful but,
Can they save me from dead,
I attained world glory fame ,
Yet all to ashes who to save me,
My life my biggest mistake,
My state my status in society,
Is like hell no one see any good,
Of me my health status is sending,
Me to the living dead my life,
Is winding up my hair has turned ,
Mad whom to save me ,
I raised children yet today no one,

Care for me my God ,
What a state am facing ,
Save me save me my God ,
Only you can save me .
Composed: by Alberto Kelly

8. Peer pressure

"Peer pressure"
Memories melodies
Might kill me
Where to start
Where to finish
What l saw granite
To be done it's cheap
As a bc let me try
They say alcohol
Es sweet than love
Yet love is sweet than
Honey honestly
I gonna know if
My friends are telling
The truth or fooling me
Take take drink
Drink drink what
Such cool pressure
I never felt before
I feel so cool
Add more and more
I feel to high take
This cigarettes too
I haven't used them
Today you gonna use
You gonna try it

Drink drink

Feeling high high
What such a pressure
I never ever tested
My life l feel paradise
Indeed you are mi true
Friends not the others
Whom say alcohol es
Not for us it's for us
From days to weeks
Taking alcohol as food
Forgetting everyone

Talking sense just
Seeing them fools
No more money
No alcohol without
Money l need to ask
My friends how
To get money
Friend go and do theft
From the old people
Also from rich people
Yeah great Idea
Let me try it
The days of one are
Numbered be careful
That were words on
Mi mind stop or you
Die give me dinero
Leave go without
Knowing l was monitored

No one can change destiny
I got a gun shot and fall down
The ground my Working up
Am behind bars
What a company what friends

Composed by Alberto Kelly

9. Tolerance

" Tolerance"
Maybe my time has
Passed no more
Of Skylark only
Is to endure end
Of time is coming
Where everyone
Wanna see what
Gonna be there
Love was mi life
But to whom to love
I was a statue on
My status mi age
Is wanting my time
Has gone indeed gone
It's time to tolerate
My state no more
Of beautiful girls
That Tibez used
To play with them
All have been taken
You alone in Esta
Universe the universe
Of wonders soon l
See being swept by
Sorrow emotions my love
True love yet today l alone
Society can't say only
Friends can hear me
No more tears down

The cheeks come on
Better days are coming
All are advice l receive
Yet l alone feel heat
Cant find one who can
Tolerate my state or
Nature want me be
Used as example to
The others only preguntas
Just let me chili wait me
Last minutes of my life
Since we are on journey
Full of ups and downs
Take me a place people
Don't stay l see my shadow
There seating seeing birds
De air and watching water
Composed by Albert Nyangaresi

10 .Be my better half

"Be my better half"
So cute stunning
From day one l saw
Paradise in your eyes
I turned to statue my love
I wonder was l dreaming
Day time yet your touches
I felt like l am your world
Looking to your little
Eyes my love l wonder
Wiii l be able to tell you
I want you in my life
I love you a lot yet l
Cant say it l am worried
Your love is one in a million
No one can be like joan
One in miles only you
Am ready to face the
Satution for you so
To see your smile my love
Only what come each
Day to my mind wiii
You deep down love
Me like l love you my baby
Wiii you be my better half
Wiii l be written in your heart
My love only time knows
All are questions that a rise
In my mind surely my Joan
Wiii she jion my journey jointly

Wiii she shine with me in my life.
Composed by Albert Nyangaresi

11. Education

" success and life "
Day in out we are yawning
Ready to suck it to be
People in tomorrow society
Not only rich ,also poor
Everyone wants education
What is education
Education education
We are working top
Tras night to be people
Tomorrow community
Mirrors of many its upon
Us education education
What wiii we get at end
We believe something es
On books ideas , wealth
We need the wealth of
Books to be top where
Our mentors are
Education education
You give us jobs
You give guidance
You inspire us to keep
Moving on with life
Education you are life
Knowledge is the key
Yet only few fellow
Knows that and working
Towards the key
Education you got no

Age not only children
Also the aged are studying
Education education
You give us men
We give you children
You give us community
Community of coordination
Education you give us love
To love ourselves and others
Education education you lit
Light to lives of those doesn't
See today es what makes tomorrow
Your deed are great
Education education
Composed by Albert Nyangaresi

12 . Minutes

"minutes"
Sunshine to my bird
She is my moonlight
The memories might
Freeze me but melodies
Of her wiii indeed kill
Me my Favourito one
I don't know when
Wiii l see my bird
That make me to
Feel eternal bond
Am tired of watching
I wanna my bird
I wanna we go
Suck nectar together
See my nest my Amor
I wanna we gonna be
We alone to this journey
I don't think l gonna do
Anything a part from
Seeing mi bird in my
Nest we gonna disfruta
Contigo from day to day
My bird am waiting
For your signal
For the joy epic
Journey we wiii
Be together tiii
Eternity no more
Of other spices

Only we alone
In the universe
Full of sweet melodies
Of love from time to time
Minutes wiii soon send
Us away to chilling
Zone more sad
Story to hear
I gut only few
Seconds now
Sun is setting
From the look
Yet l haven't said
To my bird my feelings
My bird l fear to say it
I am worried wiii
My bird go with my
Game go go
No no no
Yet my game goes
On the sun is not
Anymore
From weeks to days
Days to hours how
Things went hours
To minutes minutes
No no no
Minutes to seconds
Seconds to microseconds
So touching to hear
No say say
Wiii the bird go

Who knows the bird
Composed by Tibez Albershile

13. Melodies

"Melodies"
Tears today
Whom wiii
Wipe all the pain
She was my sunshine
So stunning Stacy
Why did l waste
Million more
Chances cautious
Can my heart be
Free from her
Indeed they
Did instigate hatred
To mi Amor and
My only love that lended
Tibez heart to hands
Memories melodies
Who wiii really tell
Her how much l miss
Her just sweet sounds
Of her melodies voice
Better to wipe all my
Story from universe
Tibez tibez
I wonder wiii l
Found like her
day in out
Only my mind is
full of questions
Indeed nothing is

more sweet like
Love she loved
Tibez body and
Soul yet end
I what did l do
Only memories
No even wrong
Message to me
Looking my mobile
Just blank but
Am optimistic on
The incoming message
Indeed this wiii be
A better lesson
Yet l do miss my
Heart surely
Wiii l see her
Even once

Composed by Tibez Albershile

14. Blame who

"Blame who "
Tell me to hear am ready,
Am tired of being mention,
Everyone each dai ,
Tibez Tibez am ready,
To hear all the statement ,
Stacy you say ,
From first day to last
Blame who
I gave you mi heart,
You see me stupid,
To be played of people,
Might not see it but you,
Knew my keys were en you,
Yet you decide to play me,
Distance dai en es problem,
Yet you can't value treasure,
Blame who
Tell me what was my ,
Mistake my moonlight,
What wrong did l do to,
To receive leftovers surely,
Am in tears timeless everyone,
Fingers to Tibez l can't manage,
This is enough even if Tibez,
Is simple as a b c l can't ,
Handle york of blame,
Blame who
All love l gave to you,
You see Tibez a toy,

To be played particularly,
Estas bien let believe it's,
Bad dream as l domir,
High for no reason hurting me,
Better to cool than to blame,
Blame who
Composed by Tibez Albershile

15.The secret admirer

"The secret admirer"
The first day l saw your
Smile l saw love in you
I thought to say l need
You but my ribs didn't
Allow me to say it
I stared at you
Like someone seen
Ghoul yet l didn't say
Anything l only muted
My mouth
Your beauty made
Me to mould metal
Picture en my heart
Yet l didn't share to
Anyone l just noticed
Your daily basis moves
Without words to say
I need you in my life
Days passed to weeks
Yet nothing l said l only
Remain Spectator ion
Despite my calmness
I didn't like anyone next
To you simply l just loved
You only mouth failed me
To shout to universe my love
For you l was now a observer
Of your tactics only Jah
Know how l had given mi key

Of my heart to you yet mi
Simplicity style was my barrier
You sounds had turned santuri
To listen to despite how days
Have gone from expressing
Heart indeed wants to have
Another one yet each time
Mouth fail us hand can write
But mouth cant speak then
Lifestyle turn to mistry only
To admirer de Encanta just
Only preguntas how many
Days weeks to pass
Even months just mind
Can't be at ease

Composed by Alberto Kelly

16. just mine

"just mine "
What l gonna give
Mi baby girl l believe
Love isn't dinero yet
La novia all need time
Contigo also love
With trust wiii Tibez
Manage that world
Only speculation l see
Yet es mi baby girl
Pounds and pesos
De Tibez l wanna give
To her and her alone
Heart and soul say
One name yet outside
There are millions
Whom wanna Tibez
Tibez is taken what
To say to them
The love l receive
I as if in world of fantasy
Impossible possible what
Love true love with
No conditions what
I gonna gift mi gift
That attained from
Mi favorite Padre
Only preguntas particular
State and steering
At her bonito

Miles planned to pay
Together as tourists
Of various places
I next to hear me en her
Heart just feeling love
No more of others
Loyalty of sand of sea
Seeking the same love
Tii the climax de earth
Composed by Tibez Albershile

17. Mi bland

"Mi bland"
Days y nouche
Tibez Albershile l have
Worked and worked
To see l myself gaining
Something of value
Not only myself also
My community y course
Mates whom Inspire me
To continue with journey
Indeed journey
Es complex yet
I have to be there
Where fellow poets
Have reached regarding
What l might face am still
Optimistic on my status.
Before surrender l have
To attain award on same
Best not better
Call me Tibez
Miles l have come
Full of hardship yet
Miles l believe going
Sky being limit success
Es my climax no of
Stories of them
Way is granite yet
I have to go through
What tragedy what

Life indeed is so
Touching to say

Composed by Albert Nyangaresi

18. Nuevo month

"Nuevo month"
It's a new month ,
Month have been ,
Waiting like bride y,
Groom month l wish,
To have a Skylark mi,
Amor to sing for me,
The month l wanna ,
Seek peace for better,
Tomorrow it's the month,
Month for better Tibez,
Month for spiritual,
Month to be en records,
Of great poets in Kenya,
Month that l wanna be,
Simple so religious ,
Cant imagine the way,
Gonna go through ,
The month to seek ,
Everything of heavenly,
The month of love ,
Month of entire adornment,
Month to understood myself,
Month of more self realization,
Indeed many things to do,
To seek knowledge prosperity,
Month where l gonna get dinero,
Month of education ,
Free month from stress,
Seeking to be loved ,

Seeking parental advice ,
To be next to my father.
Composed by Tibez Albershile

19. Desires

"desire"
Morning my mind
Is busy what to
When to start it
How to find best
Way to handle it
Only ways available
Aren't impressive
To fetch me mineral
But am optimistic
I gonna get
My desire my desire
Tomorrow l wish
Silicon so as silver
Yet to previous day
I was working for
Two diamond and
Gold what to obtain
First yet l need fame
Not just fame but
A luxury lorry to
Drive each day
My desire
What way to
Acquire all them
My desire my desire
Are increasing each
Day rapidly what to do
Whom to seek advice
My mentor l turned

Them down take me
Away away from my
Life like a joke
I haven't attained money
I need respect and power
More than my master
My desire my desire
What l gonna do
What job l gonna do
What company to be
With what should l do
Am a statue on Sunday
Yet Monday es monitoring
Me from right side what
A dilemma am facing
Reality or illusion my mind
Gonna make me mad
Composed by Tibez Albershile

20. What agony

"What agony"
When he was here ,
We thought to meet each other
With him in my mind
For both we see we are eternal
Looming beyond horizon
Playing games together
Shaking hands so touching.
When he was here
We joked jointly loved juntos
We shared bond to covalent bond
No day we cross paths
Love was love
Not love for laugh
That feeling of having one
Only one to call speak to
The touches the kiss
Memories might kill
Me my state is wanting
I wanna search but where
Looking the sky but no
Feedback for sure life
Is the greatest mistry
When one has chance
Let's utilize it .
No more of him
No more of love
No more of sweets love
Stories l used to hear
No more of this life

Better to follow him
Five fit down day time
Dead surely dead
Took even what you
Don't nor thought of

Composed by Tibez Albershile

21. I beg you

" I beg you"
I beg you
My heart mi Moonlight
You are my universe
Without you am nothing
I wanna be next to you
My heart mi heart beat
Just for you mi amor
When l beg you mi Amor
Is to continue loving me
I beg you
To feed me with love
Tiii l turn a teacher of love
Myself l don't know love
I feel to be thought love
You are my teacher de love
Don't let them chase love
We have created my love
From days to weeks mi love
Hopefully you recall mi love
I beg you
Our bond to last tiii
End of time my baby
Only l see love in you
My one love l choose
Over the million more
Cunning for my feelings
My heart my universe
I beg you don't be let
Things to end as first

As lighting l can't see
The sun shining tomorrow
I beg you
To remain mine
Alone l to be your
Student de Encanta
I to be fed by love
From mi Amor
Tii my ripe age
With my sunshine
Then l be layed
Down with mi heart
Composed by Tibez Albershile

22. Material

"Material"
Today is the start so shocking
To see a skylark from space
Ready to share with me the little portion of love to me
Making me her world she has taken security department of my heart
She doesn't need any place to stay in the ecosystem environment isn't
friendly
For that my heart is a cool and secret chamber of her to rest
So she has made me to see eternity in the new chapter in the new love
story am ready
To enter what kills me is the simplicity of her surely where
Such cute girls in this century has been held captive as slaves
Only l wonder l have to take care for my delicate daylight
No more of single now l have to mingle now many have come but she
has caught me
In the deep sea of love of loyalty so no more of cheeks
I up lift my hands so that everyone each nation
Can see she is my world the sweet soup of her l think being
Little baby of her's to suck it each day so amazing
No cute girl like her in my eyes in decades to come from today and
tomorrow
Composed by Tiberius Alberto

23. Better days are coming

"Better days are coming"
Don't surrender surely
Keep fighting keep the
Spirit better days are coming
Where we gonna have what
Others are enjoying when
We gonna be known
Of our great deeds don't
Give up it's challenge let's
Keep moving
The journey to be top
Is challenge yet we take challenge
To be known we gonna work
We have to work to be top
We have to sacrifice even soul
Just to be top we can't be
Limited at one circle circle of
Poverty no no we have to
We gonna go global l believe
We can no one is limited
Better days are coming
When our deeds gonna be
Know when people gonna
Sing our mighty deeds so
Now let's do everything to
Ensure we gonna be top
No matter if not sleeping
But you go top let's risk
Our nouche today tomorrow
We have bueno nouches

I believe we can yes we can
Better days are coming
Fast than fire and lighting
It's when we discover our
Potential today to build the
Better tomorrow to go global
It's time to impress love respect
To our elders to be there
Blessings guide one for best
Blessings are Pilar to success
Yet we gonna make effort to
Be there better days are coming
Composed by Tibez Albershile

24. Silence

"silence"
Look life like riddle
Yet feel so cool
To say so they
Gonna hear it
Shyness gonna
Erase me Tibez
Silence silence
Gonna get me
To granite tibez
Feel to say so
Sorry to say that
I won't to them to
Listen to mi story
Master of lines
Yet cero courage
What to do what
To say
Silence silence
I wish to find
Love yet l fear
Love from first
Place l wanna
Taste love yet
Mind is slow
To express it
What to say
Whom to love me
In such state
Silence silence

Teach to love
Learn to live like
Others Tibez so
You have to try
Find feelings
Confident can
Make you feel love
Try love try face
Love is sweet
Silence silence
Composed by Tibez Albershile

25. Lesson

"lesson"
Start was sweet
Sugar to lick so
Hopefully of tomorrow
Factors to remain constant
Yet my nature can't be
Changed charming
To her from her
She lit me with love
Yet two by two
To valentine fall
Was experienced
What is my love story
Shockly story to listen
From maybe my
Lifestyle can't allow
I don't think l will
Love now after all
The relationship
Failed for sure
My nature is difficult
Day in out my efforts
Are not adding value
My expectations of
Love wiii go for future
My father for
He knows one destiny
So seeing l not having
La novia is to him
No man can write his

Destiny day in out
I have put efforts
For the love story
Yet l fail from kante
To joan to tell
The fake story
Of kelcys who
Took my keys
Indeed my last
Lesson l have understood
No more love to lit
Let try something
Different from did day
Composed by Tibez Albershile

26.Gift

"Gift "
My heart you are my world whom complete me
I don't think of anything else a part from our success
I feel saying l love you alot
Bad luck l found myself speechless looking to your
Simple eyes which l have already sin my love actually
Your simplicity l wonder can l found a girl like you this century
You are my gift that almighty granted to be next with me
I feel to Compose million poetic poems for her
Her heart has actually accepted my invitation
When looking careful to her eyes l see eternity binding
Which l don't think of anyone gonna break if not almighty
Whom has granted us gift of life and love as gift to demonstrate
Day in and out l am trying to hide from my heart but where
I gonna hide actually all the keys and password she has taken
This time Tiberius Alberto has definitely found a treasure
That gonna stay with her and also of same character
Am lark witness of this love actually none ever thought of Tiberius
Alberto loving again
Only was by God wiii and Joan pretty made Tiberius statue
On looking to her pretty she made Tiberius to purelize his heart to
avoid disappointment
Composed by Albert Nyangaresi

27.Free From stress

Free from stress
It's a dream, or am day dreaming,
I never thought , that she can do all like this,
Where can I hide my face, from facing reality,
She thought me meaning of love , today she left me alone,
No word to explain, the reason behind everything,
No message that l can receive ,is like am and ruined,
Only one day l can know,the hidden Mistry behind scenes,
She has actually left me, speechless every stage of life,
She thinks leaving ,me my life wiii be miserable ,
It's so complex ,to come out from deep relationship,
But l wiii keep trying to exit this exile,
Maybe nature wanted , to apart ways ,
So no need to point fingers, but why to fake stories,
If you love someone , why you send someone else photos ,
Am worried, from when a brother be my world,
Why do you have to fake stories infront of me and my friends,
Everyone can see you, an angel but I see Satan,
No wonder , why you have not found true love,
Trust, loyalty and commitment are basic of relationship
Composed by Tibez Albershile

28. Liar

"Liar "
Just see sad story
To tell to them
Who gonna
Expect such
From someone
Who you thought
Like brother but
Chameleon of us
Actually is wanting
Am worried what
I wanna say
Call a brother
A brother joker joker
Who thought nor expect
From him but we don't
Have word to appreciate
Call judas judas
Man completely has no
Word to say thank you
First furious in making
Judgment just for
Their own benefit
Best to call buffalo
My friend my neighbour
Than him the sweet
Melodies in borrow but
The end of day story see
The amigo is lazy no reloj
Para libros esta occupado

Con esta cellular
So ironical to see
And tell story to people
Paying attention and listening
From start to climax p
Count me out
Am tired of esta life
No more no more
Chameleon in nature
Shout forget about all
Your stories behind
The scene so touching
Yet l remain dormant
Day in out for brotherhood
You see yourself perfect
May my Father forgive me
Composed by Tibez Albershile

29. Sweet betrayal

"The sweet betrayal"
So painful ,so sad to say,
I thought , she was my soulmate ,
I was actually wrong, without knowing,
Despite of how, l displayed my love toward him,
I actually turned, to be a tissue to be used by him,
I felt to flew, away but l had no wings to fly.
I never thought,of such so l was loyal,
The loyalty, has caused me to be lonely today,
The fear of losing him, turned out to be true ,
She was my inspiration, but she insticted hatred in me,
I didn't knew that she can change ,as chameleon changes its colors,
She actually ,hurt my heart.
I wonder , why I loved him so much,
I regret, dip down why did l went astray,
My best bestie , warned me but I end blocking him,
My lovely long lasting , sister warned me but I sounded rudely,
I silence, all now l am in sorrow and alone,
I thought your name pesh, is a good sign of patience ,
I never thought of holy can be so honey.
They actually ,tricked with thiny words ,
I wonder, how fast did you fall for them,
I didn't understand, where you did this but due time ,
I was able to know all that was hidden , you forgot no secret is hidden
below the sun,
It's so sad , to see the betrayal from your beloved,
Finally l find out that it's better friend , than having a lover whom for
sure is a cheater ,
I thank almighty God for his good work that he does .
Composed by Mad Poetic editor

30 . Betrayal

". betrayal"
Time told me
Yet you fooled me
They warned me
Yet l didn't listen
They advised me
Yet l did pay heed
No no no
Why all this to me
Who is there for me
Please l need help
Young and stunning
What a tragedy
I decided my time
I left mi Amor just
For mi amigos yet
I receive this painful
Story from them
I feel to flew away
Am tired of life
Pretenders are in high
Number call a liar
A liar can't soot brother
You made me ignore
My favorite maestro
Yet you are ready
To continue fooling me
No more better to die
I feel triste no more
Of stories to hear nor

Listen to l give you the
Highest honorable place
In my heart yet you hurt me
Tears down the face betrayal
By friend forever forget all
About moments we spent
Together as family
Composed by Tibez Albershile

31.Joker

"Joker"
They are busy being posting
But forgetting that about their friends and lovers
They post what even make one in tear's thinking they are doing good
Stupidity come to individual when the idea is evil
They forget about duration days spent together
They are ready to judge you without any justice
No one they can pay held to simply they think they know everything
How Can they not see light in day time seriously
I wonder what type they are and what elements that reside in them
Good in cheating when chatting
Forgetting that none is hidden from face of God
Time and season belongs to our padre
Day in out we might not see but he
Definitely see everything so
Easy as essay of eye
No need to fool a joker in the journey
Encanta is full of ups y downs
Juntos we can make it joke
A little let rest to follow after
Composed by Albert Nyangaresi

32. Cual Encanta

"Cual Encanta"
Nothing sweet like love, Nothing painful like love,
Nothing give you stress like love,
Nothing leave Tibez speechless like love,
Nothing with many memories y melodies like love,
Nothing complex to know like love,
Nothing l wanna know like love,
Nothing give me challenge like love,
Nothing l wanna speak more like love,
For Encanta Tibez l have to go miles ,
I have to understand underscore love,
Yet it's granite Tibez,
Only few wiii solve its riddle
Love one that l really love
Many have tried but all in vain,
Tibez has decided to challenge,
The chameleon Encanta
Yet am worried what is granite,
What Wii Tibez do only time,
Gonna tell when where and time,
Wiii Encanta be know ,
Miles yet feedback it's so ,
Touching even no story to heed,
Composed by Tibez Albershile

33. Sky

"Sky"
Time miles
Has given me
Best lesson ever
Even to be written
In mi heart indeed
Even l knew that
You love was true
I couldn't have played
Con you as Bublé gam
You lit me with love
Yet you gut mi ignorance
You flew away when
Wiii l re write this chapter
Tibez l turned down
When wiii l face the
Reality and erase fantasy
True love exists
Maybe l see sky
Skylark en mi sky
Back to mi world
Yet it's granite young
Stunning so cute
Gonna make you call
Her Skylark yet l see
Santuri to play to it
What a mistry Tibez
What to do when l
Gonna get guts to
Say even lo siento

Skylark es waiting es Amor
Yet you keep wasting
Million chances were
No one gonna solve
The riddle a part from Tibez
Tibez master de lines yet
So simple as a bc de Encanta
What to do you started so
Try to come with climax
More enthusiastic es true
Love nuncar end es Still there
Composed by Tibez Albershile

34. No competition

"No competition"
Am simple as simplification l wonder why you hold grudges
I don't fear from saying the universe to hear
I have no reason to hate somebody completely am a simple person
I prefer for my personality to seek peace and leave the rest
To almighty God since he is the source of all
Maybe they are seeing me a fool but my future is important for me
I can't think of anything else that might make my future futile
Better to seek peace even if is complex as cement
I wonder why some say am doing dirty work
Yet am committed continuous to see my success
Where can l start to say it from when is the right time
Am completely worried why can't they understand
My life l never and ever imagine of saying sobody
Simply l do prefer to set example to be followed
So sorry to those who can never understand me
With all what am doing day in day out
Composed by Albert Nyangaresi

35 .love y money

"Love y money"
Tell me little of love
Am a statue de love
What love what level
To say love in love
What and when you
Discover you have love
I know money matters
Most en Encanta so
Elaborate to me little
Coz am a stranger
De Encanta money
Money runs world
Then what to love
Whom gonna go
To love with lost
Guy with zero dinero
Elaborate to me l wanna
Know little de Encanta
The love we see today
Es different compared
Encanta of our abuelos
However let's empress
Little de Encanta
Money make one
To have love yet love
Isn't all about money
Zero money even interest
Of love fed and go away
Tell me does love share

Link con dinero just
Am a statue who gonna
Say that shit to me
Am in a big dilemma
What a dilemma only
Time es the best solution
Composed by Tibez Albershile

36.Free song

It's morning more
To here from Tibez
Tibez go get agua
Tibez take tea to
The farm from
The neighbours
Tibez see sleeping
Child carefully
Ensure everything
We were to take
For the journey
Are well arranged
Tibez then go
See the cow on shed
Slowly starting to get
Tired Tibez Tibez
Has turned to melody
More more and repeatedly
Tibez go water the farm
Tibez go on and call James
Am tired Tibez
Sleep today on seating room
Secure the house for
The long journey
Tibez send me toy
For my little angel
Call everyone en
The casa con abuelo
Send me a picture painting
Tibez see the pig are running

Capture them take them
Tibez all is done
There is mistake made
In the food for visitors
Tibez cook all the food
Tibez take off towel
For the visitors

Composed by Tibez Albershile

37. Padre

"Padre"
Age to age
Knows you your
Deeds are indeed
Amazing leave me
Without a say just
You are the light
That world want
Each day are looking
To seek your refugee
I wonder can l trace
A friend a father
Like you in my life
Only question on
My day in out l only
Remain image to
Be seen in each
Day mi father indeed
I feel ashamed just
When looking my
Dirty lifestyle your
Heart is full of
Mercy more than
I ever thought in
My entire life
My today tomorrow
I feel to touch
Your fit for your
To seek your
Blessings before

The world and set
Example to be emulated
By others l feel to
Serve you from
Morning tiii end of time
More interesting
Scene serving my
Padre particularly
No more listening
To anyone a part
From my father

Seeking success
Since he is alpha
Omega on everything
So l don't worry on
Anything on his
Face when year
Is a day in the eyes
Wiii l lack anything
Indeed l don't think so
Tibez padre is transcendent
So no more stories
Composed by Tibez Albershile

38. Experience

"Experience "
Tiii top miles to go ,
Libros to creo to ,
Sweet to suck fruits,
Yet the journey tiresome,
Many ways to be top,
To attain fame y power,
Yet hardship to reach,
Optimistic of satution,
We go to top of our,
Success sad to say,
How to work towards,
Success you yawn ,
Days in out no one,
Can see your pain,
Success everyone ,
Is waiting eagerly,
No advise to motivate,
You in the journey yet,
Optimistic of success,
Days in out tras nouche,
Para manana ,
Better future for,
Everyone even if ,
No support en the ,
Process you went ,
Para decades of anos,
Amigo de chameleon,
No one to help you ,
Juntos we can ,

No of it in state ,
Amor no more of,
Only mi padre ,
We gonna be there,
Full of hardships to ,
Prepare uno en life.

Composed by Tibez Albershile

39.lost

"Lost"
Tibez is lost as lost city of berbel by her beauty
I can't believe that my friend as finally find a heart
Surely man is to words and God is of actions
Never l had seen him in great joy joining me happily
I wonder which girl that as gone for his heart
I can't imagine that Tibez is known of teasing and fear
Let l believe that even impossibility is possible
With confidence confident and concentration
It's actually a good news that l have gotten
I wonder as wondering Jew how long will it take thinking of the
relationship
Nowadays no more true love it's gone lost in ages
I hope he discovers light even last stage of it
so he don't regret , l afford seeing him deep down in tears,
Mi amigo who l really value, he is mi gold ,
Tell me millions, not to leave him he is mi forever amigo,
He is completely lost, in love no of my advise he is paying heed to,
So sorry Tibez , am praying for the best,
To continue affirmative, forever tiii end of time,
Composed by Tibez Albershile

40.Blessing

"Blessings"
The success story of Tiberius,
Indeed it's awesome and amazing,
Who knows likes of kante and kelcys,
Gonna come to Tiberius Alberto ,
Story they laid indeed seed,
For future which decades ,
That comes and goes the efforts ,
Can't be forgotten ,
Indeed it's blessings.
Just it's online where Tiberius ,
Meant such powerful mentors,
Despite how life is still the deeds,
For individual can't be forgotten ,
Where Tiberius is story gonna ,
Be narrated future days ,
Then like of kelcys and Kante,
Vital role must mentioned,
Where no hope was seen ,
Still you instigated to believe ,
Better days are coming ,
Indeed it's a blessing.
Jah is just beyond
Season so awful
Young age so powerful
Words to inspire not
One but many not
Same society but she is social
So impressive to see ladies
For the century still firm to

Support fellow youths
To attain dreams and desires
Indeed it's a blessing.
Composed by Tibez Albershile

41. Flower

"Flower"
Its blossom indeed its a great ,
Flower we gonna get what ,
A great generation gonna be,
The species gonna disfruta ,
Con esta flower the bee ,
Are just waiting the end,
Of the bud stage and utilize,
The opportunity to fullest ,
The great flower, the great flower.
It's morning more love,
The farmer for first activity,
For the day is to sprinkle water,
De flower water is basis of life,
What awesome scene who ,
Can't like to see the flower,
The plant has taken years ,
Yet farmers still optimistic ,
The better days are coming ,
When harvest gonna be bien ,
The great flower, the great flower.
The long waiting is soon gonna end,
Smile of farmer surely support this,
Time has gone since that smile was,
Seen the sunshine indicating everything ,
Gonna be bien why not to smile,
Climate es favorable de farming,
The flower and other plants gonna,
Grant the farmer more money indeed,
The great flower, the great flower.

What a ruin why to start ,
Where to finish everything,
Has gone to mess what agony ,
Time dedicated day in out ,
Sleepless night nothing out ,
Can't believe maybe am day ,
Dreaming yet it's reality can't ,
Believe better to be five fit,
Deep down the ground ,
Indeed it's a great agony,
The great flower, the great flower.
Composed by Tibez Albershile

42. The Cold night

"The cold night "
Night for two why now two
When l gonna get mine
Time has indeed gone
To sad to tell still no one
The cold night gonna
Killi me where are you
My state is not good the view
Is wanting it need your
Support the cold nouche
Night for two
Night to feel high night
Am longing to see it's
Cold night where we
Put love to reality it's
The cold nouche where
We feel the feeding
The real love that is
Hidden that bear eyes
Can't see it's cold nouche
To see the mountains
To suck sweetness from
Honey it's cold nouche
Night for two
Two birds of same feathers
Ready to see magic of cold
Nouche nouche it's indeed
Nouche for dos la novia
What to say where is
Mi amor to see the mistry

Of love it's indeed cold nouche
Deep down ready to suck
The soup to feel little tight
Deep down it's the cold
Nouche where the scenes
Aren't so appealing
Yet it's fantastic nouche
Night for two
Indeed l wanna test the cold night
To see the mistry of mountains
To taste the soup for first time
Many have tried and more
Appealing it's the cold night
See the moon monitoring
Isn't so scary so l wanna
Feel to be fed little of love
On the season de cold nouche
Night for two.
Composed by Tibez Albershile

43.unity amongst humanity

Name : Ashok Chakravarty Tholana
Country: India
Poem Title: unity amongst humanity
Whenever I write poetry
It makes my mind totally free,
The inspiration it confers ...
With my joy; never it differs.
Poetry can please anyone
Poetry can transform anyone,
It promotes peace and amity,
To dispel the element of enmity.
Devoid of caste, creed and religion,
Poetry loves to live in any region,
It stands for justice and equality,
Aspires for unity amongst humanity.
Inviting a volley of ideas mature
Without any barriers of culture;
Poetry is a weapon of serenity,
Can defuse thoughts of animosity.
With compassion-filled words
Let every poet pacify the world,
Poetry is something worthful,
That's powerful and purposeful.
Copyright©AshokChakravarthyTholana

44. A grim struggle

A grim struggle
Time, peels-off the charm
Stirs inconceivable storms,
Life experiences something,
Ultimately it loses everything,
Indeed, it's the character of life.
The hands of time are pitiless
Advancing life feels the mess;
In the wheel of time, it shuttles,
Leaving memories just to ruffle,
Birth to death, it's a grim struggle.
@ Dr. Ashok Chakravarthy Tholana
Poet-Writer-Reviewer
Hyderabad,
Telangana State, INDIA

45.together we can ....

"together we can"
If we promote unity
We can find real humanity,
If we promote peace
We can find real solace,
If we promote harmony
We can dispel human agony,
If we promote love
We can find a joys trove.
If we promote prosperity
We can easily detach enmity,
If we promote friendship
We can get rid of all hardship,

Every war has inflicted pain
With death and destruction,
In the vortex of selfishness
We lost the element of uprightness,
By keeping away from peace
We are struggling to find solace,
And by ignoring human rights,
We are feeding the vultures of hate.
Yes, together .....
Let's create an ambiance of amity
That strengthens the bond of unity,
Without falling prey to perpetrators,
Without falling prey to dictators;
Let's fortify and uphold peace,

Yes, together we can make peace.
copyright@AshokChakravarthyTholana

46.The Ring

"The ring "
When to wear it whom
Gonna put on my finger
Say mine tiii end of time
Am statue all amazing
All l knew all l was found
Of all are gone all gone
Can't believe nor imagine
The ring , the ring .
I feel to be one feeling
The same moments to
Wear it on my finger to
Say sweet simple so
Amazing word that crowd
Gonna love and laugh
To just mi Amor
Surely it's a fantastic scene
Everyone waiting to see it
The ring , the ring .
It's bound by promises
The ring linking two souls
The ring making start of new
Family faithful life what
Awesome scene people
See it granite some see
Simple as a bc the ring that
People work for decades
The ring , the ring.
Indeed it's something to be
Written down in books the

Amazing ring that rung
Inside our minds and heart
The ring of saying adios to single
Lifestyle to impress family style
The ring makes joy to society
It's the same ring that gives us
Tears the ring we should keep
The ring to it's rightful place
The ring of new chapter new story,
The ring , the ring.
Composed by Tiberius Alberto

47. Count down

" count down "
What a society what a community,
The century indeed it's counting ,
Down the line even l only wonder,
As wondering jew on summer season ,
Whom gonna save this society ,
This generation ,
Indeed its wanting only ,
God knows the wiii of man,
Let us count the count down.
Technology technology ,
Indeed has brought impressive ,
Things to our century however ,
Tears down the cheek whom,
Gonna be there next ,
Generation to come only ,
Preguntas en mi mind ,
Whom gonna be mirrors,
Whom gonna educate our ,
Children call help to who,
Technology technology ,
Let us count the count down.
Innovation and creativity ,
Indeed is tears down cheek ,
Whom to think beyond box,
What gonna next generation ,
Do technology has killed ,
Us not just us but society ,
Changes are indeed impacting ,
Society negative what agony ,

Can't believe indeed tears ,
Let us count the count down.
Our minds are becoming,
So limited cant imagine ,
Still we are young why,
To stop such mentality ,
Indeed is a painful scene ,
To see and watch where ,
We heading to indeed ,
We see tears down the line ,
Let us count the count down.
Composed by Tibez Albershile

48. World Earth

"Indeed it's earth "
What amazing wow
Sky is shining amazing
This is indeed home
Home for everyone
The plants and animals
Home for living and non living
Home for everyone
Indeed it's earth.

The swing of plants
The best scene on sky
Can't imagine even think
Indeed it's awesome earth
The sunshine gonna cut
Us with vitamin d body
Indeed is growing so
Health and awesome
Can't believe the Fresh
Air with the equilibrium
Rain that indeed make
Our maize and many
Plants
Indeed it's earth.
A cooling place not
Just living but also
Non living thing the
Elements of nature

Make earth home for
Everything not just
Home but best place
To stay for many anos
To come and go indeed
Its a home cant imagine
The other planets
Indeed it's earth
Let myself to be a stammer
But not being silent from
Speaking fact and figures it's
Enthusiastic scene to narrate
To be written where everyone
The future generation to come
To read so no any information
Gonna be left out can't imagine
Narrating bit by bit of it
Indeed it's earth home for all
Indeed it's earth .
Composed by Alberto Kelly

49. Promise

"promise"
Take mi money mi heart
I am ready to give mi life
Down just to see how l
Love you see mi amor
I wanna go no where l
Wanna just joke and enjoy
Peaceful moments with
Mi amor
Life it's a gift mi Amor
Yet l promise to give
Out to you am ready
To give mi comida just
To see mi Amor satisfied
Nothing more nothing less
Just to see smile what
Amazing scene on a
Full moon night with mi
Moonlight mi Amor
Mi amor
Your value my baby
It's on in million miles
That we are going for good
For me and you my love
I only need to see
A smile my Skylark
Nothing more nothing less
You beautiful eyes make
Me to provide you each
Moment each time

Mi amor
Five fit ground gonna
Be reason for end
De Encanta less
Than that l don't think
So you are mi world
Am your slave for
Your love l feel even
To sing mi love to see
How melodic l am
Tibez Tibez indeed
I wanna all mi pesos
To be given
To mi amor.
Composed by Tibez Albershile

50. The hand

"The hand"
The hand that handed
The heart honorably
The hand that you hurdle
Recklessly
The hand that used to
Write well presentable
Poems
The hand granted you pesos
Same hand is given out
The hand.
Ready to do right
Things just to justify
You the hand that tiii
The earth to see
Food on the table
The hand that handed
You to parents you
Discover from day
One the hand to be
Trust worth not
Just playing with you
Same hand you spoil
The hand.
Cut it cut it down
Cant see it anymore
The hand that give
You place you title
The same hand
You just used as

Bridge you leave it
The hand that give
You pure and sacrificial
So humbled honestly
Dedicated love
The hand.
Love of money love
To tiers down the cheek
The love of fame fake love
Love of dinero isn't love
The love lost the loyalty
The love that led to end
The love which l was warned
To hand in her hand
I ignored to hand her
To everyone the same hand
The hand .
Composed by Tibez Albershile

51. Satisfied with mi work

" Satisfied with mi work"
Morning more awesome
Ready to make my daily
Routine to seek dinero
So punctual so to ensure
Mi familia gonna get
At least comida
What inspire me alot
Mi fellow friends whom
By the earlier bird are
School teaching to
Impressive.
The worker.
The doctors are ready in hospital
To treat patients and ensure the
Society gonna have health living
Standard without forgetting the
Police officers in whom maintain
Law and order for the wellbeing
Of the society indeed society
Give rise to children to serve
The society in future for sure
It's a impressive occasion
To see and witness
The Worker
The society is brought by religious
Way of living by various leaders
The various values make the society
Can't imagine the role the work
Of the church , the church leaders

Whom ensure we grow spiritual
Mental for many miles we gonna
Go for generations to come
The worker.
The poets are busy composing
Writing the written scripts for
The future generation to see
The knowledge as key to success
Gonna go also to future generations
They aren't limited from saying
The good also condemning the evil
The earn living just from writing
Society is inspired from writing
Nation is built by the writers
The worker .
Composed by Alberto Kelly

52 . It's hiv and aids

"hiv and aids"
dead is real not illusi
on ,
The infection isn't illusion ,
Brother , sister are suffering ,
Why suffering why agony ,
No one knows the reason ,
The illness no brother, no sister,
It's HIV and AIDS .
It's has come as results,
Of ignorance of us,
Inheritance of wife,
The butching of meat ,
During hunting day in ,
Out without consideration ,
It's finishing the society ,
Whom gonna see future ,
Whom gonna tell ,
The effect of it,
It's HIV and AIDS .
The infection deep down
Knows no friend nor enemy
The virus has finished villages
The infection has infected
Not only poor but also rich
See now it has no friend
At all pay heed to stop
It since what has cause
Can't miss solution so
Settle seek advice at

Early stages
It's HIV and AIDS .
HIV and AIDS has no cure,
No cure no cure yet some,
Means are brought to help man,
To have health status ,
When the disease is discovered ,
At early stages so stop ,
Shyness seek medication ,
Seek treatment to see,
Tomorrow together we ,
Gonna go far no man ,
On his own island lets ,
Impress the spirit ,
It's here to stay to settle
With us
It's HIV and AIDS .
Composed by Tibez Albershile.

53.cyclic Encanta

" Cyclic Encanta"
Love love the dynamic Encanta
The love of golden age is this
Fresh in people mind only
Preguntas people have they
Erase the error of massagers
So fast as lighting so sorry
Maybe no one recall the same
The cyclic Encanta.
The love of juntos to see
Hermano having mujer de choice
No more or am day dreaming
Cant imagine how fanny it was
Just it was matter of monitoring
Waiting for best chance to do
Capture , re capture and love
Story start from simple background
Tiii the complex de marriage
The cyclic Encanta.
The silly so simple la novia
Where did they flew to worries
The one interested con comida
So determine to enter Encanta
Provided comida estas available
Where when we gonna meet
Such soul why the soul
Being traced is granite cant
Imagine nor think beyond
The cyclic Encanta.
Gut nothing but gut a rose

De mi Amor wanna spend
Mi life con mi Amor just
To see the smile on mi Amor
Estas adequate just gut a rose
The rose just sigh de Encanta
I adore mucho mi Amor
The little gut l gonna spend
Contigo mi Amor where did
Estas Encanta went
The cyclic Encanta.
Love love the error de dinero
Poor soul such as us whom
Gonna see our true love
The cyclic Encanta is making
Young to take risk to see
In love the fake Encanta only pesos
Can't think little de Encanta
The fake statement , stories
Just de dinero no dinero no Encanta
Biggest challenge , en Encanta journey
The cyclic Encanta.
Composed by Tibez Albershile.

54. Am tired

" Am tired"
Can't wait , can't wait
Am tired , am tired
Why all the waiting
When to see her smile
When to see sunshine
When to lit love on her
Am tired, am tired.
Tell mom , tell dad
Am tired , l wanna her
Tell friends, am tired
Am tired of cold night
I wanna her, l wanna
To feel her am high
Yet no young to interact
So sorry to say
Am tired, am tired.
Sky can see clearly
The moon watching me
At nouche y sun at day
The way am feeling myself
I wanna to see her the one
I see in mi dreams the one
Ripe just as Bananas
One of values for real
Am tired, am tired.
When to mark long wait
Over when to see her
Why to wait all the time
Soon l gonna shift

Am l waiting for gold
An waiting for diamond
Am waiting for silver
Then what am waiting
Love , oooooh love
The eternal love
However my interest
Soon are fading away
Am tired, am tired.
Composed by Tibez Albershile.

55. Just a minute

" just a minute"
Mi love mi love
Why all why this
Just a minute alone
Mi sunshine Stacy
I wanna just a minute
To say little sense
Just a minute.
Can't imagine nor thought
The many promises , mi love
My Skylark , one for life,
Even a single one
Grant me just a minute
I feel to express mi pain
My tears down the cheek
The pain of being broken
Loving wrong person
Just a minute.
All we said to each other
All the time we spend
Shaking hands , hags
Can't imagine , all is gone
To shift with someone else
Wiii l manage wiii l love anyone
Just as l deed to you
Only preguntas , even erasing
You is granite mi Amor
Just a minute.
I feel to feel your love
Just for once , to be next

To my love hearing sweet
Melodic sounds listening santuri
Just watching the birds juntos
However it's complex
It's so sorry to say to Migos
Just a minute
Minute might re write broken
Love that lost to wall of earth
Just a minute.
Composed by Tibez Albershile

56. No more cry

"No more cry "
I deeply thank jah, after all l receive,
My heart is pure , more healed to start,
A new story , however no clue de story,
Thanks to mi lost Amor, she lit little light,
Two days, before she flew away ,
Now l have attained , knowing to know,
The fake love stories, the true love story,
No more cry.
I lost a treasure, however God gave me title to be a poet,
Through my works, l have my fans we
Grow together ,
Can't imagine how things were, can't think the way l felt
All isn't it's gone , thanks to Sir Jah ,
The blessings l receive is beyond limit,
Where am today no one , thought nor imagine of only Sir Jah ,
No more cry.
Love is sweet as honey indeed to lick,
However try the Love of Sir Jah ,
Indeed you gonna feel eternal love,
Eternity bond no more cry for love
Broken for love chase true love , the love
That this century , can't see with eyes,
The infinity love , love beyond measures,
The true love , for life cant wait to be there to test the love,
No more cry.
Cry is for weak however even war warriors do cry
The pain of being played by love
The pain of losing one of members
Not cry for Encanta each day that

Dynamic or the error came to pass
The cry when poverty , when to be top
The cry for this error
No more cry.
Composed by Tibez Albershile.

57. My story

" My story "
When l think little of myself ,
I thank God for only one who,
Knows myself , my story for real,
My ups and downs no one ,
Gonna understand , better,
Than my God , my father ,
It's my story .
My story my lifestyle cant,
Imagine nor think of little,
Where l have come the ,
Hardship the struggle , all today,
Am here can't believe , the society
The society that , ready to bury me ,
Cant believe it's God,
It's my story .
The best friends l found ,
For real l can't forget ,
The day l meet Dan my friend ,
For real is more than a brother ,
Come my ups and downs we ,
Are together help each other ,
All is to Sir Jah through Vincent,
My story to be read to society,
It's my story .
No one is safe from love ,
Love the greatest mistry ,
Not just poets alone all,
Fall Infront of love the love ,
Just like l felled to false love,

That I was played as soccer ,
To sorry to say that my love,
Was so true and pure as purity ,
However it ended in tears ,
It's my story .
It's my story my life ,
No one knew me only Jah,
When everyone time ended ,
I remained with Jah it's my ,
Sad story to many it's a good ,
Lesson to many whom gonna listen,
To my story , to change for future,
It's my story , that consist facts,
It's my true story , that I have gone,
It's my story .
Composed by Mad poetic editor

58.beautiful are yet to be born

" beautiful are yet to be born"
Tell me ready to hear
Keep mi word l wonder
Which world am l in
The beautiful faces
I see gonna cut me
From mi favorito one
Joan just what about
The others
The beautiful are yet to be born.
Can't imagine nor think
Little of the say one
I just gotten l feel l got gold
Am gonna be full no other
Wants however human wants
Are always endless
Why l stiii doubt my mind
My body what l gonna do
However the one l have
Attain to on mi hands can't
Allow her to flew away
The beautiful are yet to be born.
Indeed the pretty one
Are on the way to be home
Inspire of the way to home
Just am fully taken by mi favorito
Captured in capture re capture
Can't return back from the continent
De sugar and honey to bitter herbs
Can't even imagine , nor think of

Such day en mi life the love
Indeed l receive idea beyond measure
Even weighing machine may fail
To measure accurate
The beautiful are yet to be born.
The soul and body are save
The home l dwell l feel to stay
To see beautiful l hear about
The name joan is just start of
The journey de Encanta yet
I hear beautiful to be born can't
Imagine nor think little of it
The beautiful that mi Amor
The pretty than mi Amor
No no no tiii end of time
She es one in a million
The beautiful are yet to be born.
Composed by Tibez Albershile.

59. My life in agony

"Mi life in agony"
Father mother are pillars
Good family good society
Good society good nation
What agony what am l not
Seeing where are we heading
Whom gonna save us
Each day it's fight
Fight fight
Which generation , which society,
Are we building up , l wonder what,
I gonna do, no one is weak to humble,
The husband as head, the woman neck,
The children are busy watching
They are worried what they gonna do
They can't stand any side ,so sorry
If choose father, for the motherly love,
Gonna despite from same day ,
Choosing mother , might be seen stupid,
Some state are dilemma day in out
No day , no peace at home
The fight is making things hard
There is exam to revise , the peaceful,
Environment indeed it's needed, to whom,
To humble , to whom to see value of peace,
Both are high in tempers to sorry to see
No peace no peace at all
Home is best all time however
This case home is hell
Seek place seek peace

Tired of fight for each day
Wanna place wanna peaceful
Scene l gonna see smile
On my face l wanna see
Peace cansado de fight
No peace no peace
What values impacting to generations
Cansado better away from home
Than hell in home .
Composed by Alberto Kelly

60.king of hearts

"king of hearts"
King of hearts , king of hearts ,
Am tired , am tired what love ,
What love , am tired of love ,
King of hearts , king of love ,
Come snach , your heart,
Am tired of love, king of love,
What mistake, what crime deed
I deed to face such fate , king de love
Did l failed with ancestors, king of hearts
Did l fall in love with wrong girl
Why each day , each time same
Story king of hearts , am tired
The love l see, the love l read ,
The are two different types king of hearts,
Can't l get tips, can't l know mi mistakes,
King of love then teach me, tell me love,
Many good l have seen , l have interacted,
However l failed to do my part , which part,
I failed to understand , l failed to know,
Since such love l read , in poems aren't reality,
King for love, king of hearts grant me tips,
To excel in love ,
They see you as king of hearts, king of love,
You know all love, you have underscored love,
Why can't l be like you king of love, to gain such titles,
However l need to explore love , to understand love ,
To be next with king de hearts and king de love .
Composed by Mad poetic editor

61. Questions

" Questions"
Life lessons are best,
Tibez am pondering,
Mi mind con preguntas,
When what to say actually,
Life like riddle life of centuries,
The life of this century am jew,
What l gonna do when ,
I gonna get my audience ,
To do even spoken word ,
For first time only preguntas .
Thanks God l got best poets,
We gonna do collaboration
Poets like Job , Rovie whom are right,
Next to meet , want to drop new pieces
So society can be influenced, so amazing,
To see stiii poetry is a inspiration tii ,
This century despite platos past arguments,
Poets are building the centuries , for
Indeed centuries coming,
Gonna get best poetry , booklet to inspire,
Such soul to walk to write part, only then,
Another challenge arise , how many to reach,
How many gonna get , your knowledge,
Many lack smart phones, many don't like to listen to spoken words,
People are tired of poetry , people see as
Wastage of time
Only questions in my mind.
Then who gonna liberate , this century
The don't heed to advice, they don't want

To waste time , searching information in books just to enjoy
What methods , what way the message
Gonna reach everyone ,
Cant worry for publishment , Amazon it's the best for free,
How many gonna get time to pay visit to Amazon website ,
Only question with no answers.

Composed by : Mad poetic editor

62. Just your heart

" Your heart "
Mi favorito one , mi best one
What to say , to you for real
Even l am surprised, to say it,
It is too early to say , Silvia however,
The early bird, catches the worm,
You are the worm, and Kelly is the bird
Targeting your heart, l need nothing more,
Just your heart.
For this life l have interacted , with many good ,
Sweetness of loading , such likes you know them,
However Kelly has seen , Silvia heart so special ,
Just for Kelly alone, nothing more nothing less,
Just l gonna be satisfied , when l gonna get the heart,
Just your heart.
Why you , yet l just meet you of late,
No one can write is fate, fate is one for,
Real wanna Kelly to chase your heart, just nature is the middle men,
To ensure we meet , why to create the the barrier,
For all what happens it is wiii , of our father ,
Sky is high for real, your heart is my home to settle on the sky,
Just your heart.
Got many Migos , whom gonna gave it,
My heart my mind, wanna one name one,
La novia for life , for sure Silvia your heart,
Gonna get me in trouble , but can not avoid trying,
We used to shy the , error of shyness ,
Flew away no more , we now express ,
Openly out our feelings, no need to hide,
Just your heart.

God grants, gifts and fruits to various ,

People to me your heart, l see it as my gift ,

That l gonna treasure my lifetime, can not deny that,

Let the universe hear the same, your heart it only what l want,

To hear from you , y only you con your heart ,

To listen to melodies sounds , de lips de Silvia each minute,

Just your heart.

Composed by Mad poetic editor

63. Fame

" Fame"
No one is left , to my right to my left,
Everyone wanna be known, not just know,
To get honor , tittle what society,
What nation we are building am a statue,
Looking little of my society, my individual,
Only preguntas the fame gonna, led us to hell,
Why fame , what after all fame .
The are many ways, many styles to attain,
Nothing come on silverly Plata, most ways are with a price,
Choose the cheapest way , which you gonna pay heavily,
Just fame not even youths are safe, what so surprising,
To see the wisdom of community, searching for fame,
So touching indeed , however it's life,
Why fame , what after all fame .
Life need to progress , life needs to move on,
Whether you have nor , you luck but life needs to kick,
Which path to choose , the path for dinero,
The path for honestly , honestly comes also with price,
Being honestly for nothing, tii end up to humbled background,
Choose shortcut , never know when how things,
Gonna go astray , when the table turn,
Why fame , what after all fame .
Fame is sweet as sugar, so impressive to see yourself ,
With big honor ,big tittle big things ,
All in the name of fame, what does come in mind ,
When one is five fit down the ground, wiii fame save you,
When your soul separate , from your body
Wiii same fame save the soul, search then heavenly fame,
The eternal fame , the fame without end,

Why fame , what after all fame .
Composed by Mad poetic editor

64. Last minute de Encanta

"last minute of Encanta "
The one you choose , the one you take,
She is taken , the one you feel bond,
You see love , you feel to be yours,
She is taken , maybe mi last minute,
De Encanta , Kelly l have shifted,
To right , to left what l see it's,
History repetition,
last minute of Encanta .
When to get one, where to trace,
One you see simple, soul you have ,
Traced to sorry, to hear soul gone,
Why each day each time , Kelly why ,
Tears down the cheek, no one can hear,
My pain my hurts , my wounds deeply,
They say nothing hurts , nothing pains ,
More than Encanta , indeed. Love it is
So painful weapon , can affect anyone,
last minute of Encanta .
No man , no women is safe for me real,
Those you choose today, watch them keenly,
Those giving you hopes , watch them keenly,
No one knows, no one expects to see changes ,
Watch them closely , be like one y shadow ,
For real that gonna be, best weapon,
Leave them free , to do paddock. , you gonna recall,
You gonna cry , guide such souls value them,
last minute of Encanta .
No more Encanta , no more Encanta,
It is high time , high time to do something,

More big , more hurt gonna hurt your heart,
Each day relax , focus to come up ,
With global project, people to feel ,
Your pain , your hurts taking hands,
Towards the wrong vessel , to fetch water,
No more Encanta , no more Encanta,
Time for dinero, time for mi amigos,
Cansado et aburrido , only mi padre ,
Gonna determine, mi next steps mi next stage ,
last minute of Encanta .
Composed by Mad poetic editor

65. Last minute of Encanta

"last minute of Encanta "
The one you choose , the one you take,
She is taken , the one you feel bond,
You see love , you feel to be yours,
She is taken , maybe mi last minute,
De Encanta , Kelly l have shifted,
To right , to left what l see it's,
History repetition,
last minute of Encanta .
When to get one, where to trace,
One you see simple, soul you have ,
Traced to sorry, to hear soul gone,
Why each day each time , Kelly why ,
Tears down the cheek, no one can hear,
My pain my hurts , my wounds deeply,
They say nothing hurts , nothing pains ,
More than Encanta , indeed. Love it is
So painful weapon , can affect anyone,
last minute of Encanta .
No man , no women is safe for me real,
Those you choose today, watch them keenly,
Those giving you hopes , watch them keenly,
No one knows, no one expects to see changes ,
Watch them closely , be like one y shadow ,
For real that gonna be, best weapon,
Leave them free , to do paddock. , you gonna recall,
You gonna cry , guide such souls value them,
last minute of Encanta .
No more Encanta , no more Encanta,
It is high time , high time to do something,

More big , more hurt gonna hurt your heart,
Each day relax , focus to come up ,
With global project, people to feel ,
Your pain , your hurts taking hands,
Towards the wrong vessel , to fetch water,
No more Encanta , no more Encanta,
Time for dinero, time for mi amigos,
Cansado et aburrido , only mi padre ,
Gonna determine, mi next steps mi next stage ,
last minute of Encanta .
Composed by Mad poetic editor

66.Poet feelings

" poet feelings"
What scene to see a poet in love ,
Ready to write many ,more awesome ,
Poem just for the lover ,
Ready to play ,with words to impress ,
The lover just like any person ,
Gonna do to impress the girlfriend ,
The poet feelings.
Gave heart openly ,and requested ,
Nothing just, to honor the love ,
Keep the miles, to be just loyal,
To the lover however human ,
Stiii are human, can't change at all,
No matter how, loyal you are still ,
You gonna be played,
No matter how ,close you are you,
Gonna feel the hit ,
The poet feelings.
It's so sad to say to tell,
People to listen ,to the painful ,
Story of the scene, of what occurred ,
However creative and imaginative,
Poet can play, the best in that part ,
Only what he needs just paper and pen,
To transform , the betrayal to best poem,
To inspire many , however to leave on in tears ,
The poet feelings.
When loved , why to play with feelings ,
When loved can't you settle , to see love
Completely can't understand, stop ups and downs,

Just enjoy to be loved , to hear poems
To give your lover, tips to write to
The society that waiting , to see new poem,
The poet feelings.

Indeed poets are some shy to say,
Too shy to say best to arrange words
To best order to evoke , catastasis feelings,
To less of speaking too many lines being composed in mind,
To sad to be broken by love, to happy for good readers gonna,
Get new pieces for the break up, the broken up of poet
Too awesome to see poet in love, too amazing to see poet broken,
The poem to be given to society are so impressive,
The poet feelings.

Composed by Mad poetic editor

67.One day

" One day "
One day l gonna sleep ,
Eternity sleep , can not imagine,
One day l gonna , go to visit my padre,
Whom you gonna hurt, whom you gonna,
Talk to just one day , l gonna say bye,
When l have done, with all my writing,
When l gonna have , no barrier on earth,
Just one day , just a day.
Think the loyalty of me, think how a cared,
Ready to be even you cheek, not losing you ,
Think all the best moments we, have spent together,
Despite of how life is, nothing is permanent ,
Our lives are at his hands , no one knows tomorrow ,
One day like this , l gonna be paradise ,
Just one day , just a day.

When l gonna say adiós, to my favorite ,
Poetry mi daily routine, at least two poems,
In a day imagine of , one day we gonna be water and paraffin,
We can not meet despite , of how bond we shared,
It is so sorry to my friends for life, for real the life,
Gonna be granite our covalent bond, gonna break,
Just one day , just a day.
No one knows , even l do not know,
When where , the incident gonna happen,
My days are now numbered, reaching hundred Years ,
Gonna be a great mistry , my fellow poets,

Whom you gonna , request for collaborative poems,
Whom gonna be there , when Kelly gonna be out ,
Utilize me , utilize me no one knows tomorrow,
Just one day , just a day.

When we hear a call, we all respond ,
When we respond to call, that marks
The climax of our story, my love make me feel loved,
Just a day like this moment like this, tears gonna be in your cheeks,
Do not waste chance at hand, my friend lets enjoy together,
One time in life you gonna gather, you gonna say byee byee Kelly,
One day in life l gonna be all the platforms, people to hear me,
Posted farewell brother, farewell fellow poet,
Today no one gonna post , Even my project no one needs me
Just one day , just a day.
That minute you gonna need me, the most,
That time an know by my poems, my plays ,
That time you gonna search me, only memories,
You gonna get, the Republic had greatest ,
Poet bad luck , no one is safe, from dead,
Kelly is gonna with , the creativity best ,
Lines of Kelly gonna be , remembered
Just one time in life , when the dark phase,
Gonna take Kelly for , eternity rest finishing up the inspiration work,
It's one day in life l wiii be known.
Just one day , just a day.
Composed by Mad poetic editor

68.The one I gut

"The one l gut "
Indeed it is a gold , need nothing ,
The sweetness, the actions,
Indeed are amazing , the la novia,
Kelly got is really amazing,
She gonna, teach Kelly Encanta,
For Kelly has , longed to know Encanta,
The chance that , he was waiting ,
It is at hand it high time, Kelly to feel,
The one Kelly got, is one in million.
She knows more , de Encanta,
Come to Kelly , knows nothing,
Kelly knows best , lines in best order,
What a surprise, many levels Kelly,
Has been now High level, yet no nothing,
De Encanta , can not imagine nor believe,
Kelly soul es pure , white as snow,
He gonna put trust con esta, nuevo la novia,
The one Kelly got, is one in million.
Kelly necessito , no one no dinero,
Kelly heart has been hurt, has been used,
In a wrong way, now moment it is here,
Kelly world class poet, to know Encanta,
Wow it is amazing to hear, to see Kelly,
One of the best, best poet , best writer,
Wanna know Encanta , so awesome so many love poems,
The one Kelly got, is one in million.

Surely even poets do face, challenge in love,
What a scene , the best poet all time,
Face difficult to his , own field his world,
Feel to laugh , what a satution on a hot,
Sunday summer day , when Kelly wanna,
Move towards the journey , de Encanta ,
So amazing , need some doves ,
Needs some regalo , to surprise Sophie,
To teach Kelly Encanta, for real Kelly ,
Wanna know , step by step ,
Tiii the final stage , the one Kelly gut,
Gonna be helpful to Kelly,
The one Kelly got, is one in million.
So impressive , not Kelly chooses,
Anyone anywhere , no at all Kelly,
Had seen for real something, so simple,
Soul that can not be seen, not be traced,
To this century , the century of dynamic,
So cute but humble, l really wonder ,
Kelly found such soul , where and how,
The shy Kelly , the simple Kelly ,
Only questions with little answers,
The one Kelly got, is one in million.
Composed by: Mad poetic editor

69.Beyond the Threshold

"Beyond the Threshold"
Where have you been so far?
Or are you living like a made man, chasing nothing everywhere?
Have you gone somewhere?
Or are you still the way you're?
You need to prosper.
You need to prosper.
Make your current version a better,
For you to become stronger,
Many have left you forever
And you will never dwell together
But their leaving gives you a chance
To rediscover, and shine more brighter
In the nick of time, you can be a changer
So that everyone will suddenly remember
That you are the one who makes without fear
A beacon of hope, a shining light clear
You are a man of letters,
Share your ideas with sincerity and care.
Share your ideas with the world outside, my dear,
For if you do so, they won't call you a truth teller.
But rather, with those untrustworthy people, you'll be compared,
And your words will be weighed, with a skeptical air.
Composed By *AZB*Ahmad zaji bunu

70.My heart for life

" My heart for life"
I was busy thinking of love
Thinking of how to express my love
How to put my words in the
right place.
How to convince a heart
to see how much I truly love
Looking forward to hear a reply
But what did I get in return?
I can't love
You are not my class
You can't tolerate me
You can't bear my actions
You can't treat my fake up
You will be tired of me when the time comes
Is this all you can say?
I wanna hear more from you
Do you think, I fall for you because I can't accept all this?
Then you are wrong.
My heart for life , my heart for life.

No matter how many times, love hurt, breaks and cause you pain never
stop loving....
Try the best you could to embrace true love.
The sky is the limit, your love is my home,
Your bond can not think , nor imagine ,
Day with my Skylark, l feel to say to shout,
So everyone , on earth can feel our Encanta,

My sunshine , mi santuri only l fear ,
My honey what l gonna say, your un conditional love,
For real your, my lifetime bird,
I gonna shield that heart, l gonna be with my heart,
Tiii the end of time , my heart for Life
The gift , that l got from God,
My heart for life , my heart for life.
I caught myself writing this love pics... Is a direct msgs.
Created by : Content Artist

71. Am gone

"Am gone"
This too shall end
Just push always to the end
happy are they who defend
like the roots to withstand
One day is coming,
The flowers will flourish
For a victor to perish,
He who the world cherish
My leaves are so pale,
But many are they in the lane
The path is not plain,
others says it is stained
The stems are cut off,
My lamb is almost dying off
all should not shy off,
but let the candle put off
I must say goodbye ,
but its to early to say it by
My ailment should cast me by,
The tomb the grave stay by
I plead with you
Do not carry a awe,
nor share with the whore
The cistern of the weak owe
Those leaves are fading
So my life is ending
Continue the passion toasting
When it's time I should be going
I have failed you much

To the end I could not match
So early I quite the march
Before my birthday in March
Forgive me my darling
my friends as I am parting ,
hold on to the end journing
because soon we are winning

By Bande Job
24-05-2024

72. Why Me

"Why Me"
What to say, where to start,
The affection , the care is gone,
Whom to tell, whom to listen,
Memories and melodies,
When l recall such scene,
Feel to cry , the sweet love,
That l received , in name of friendship,
Today is gone, gone forever can not,
Imagine even little , little of it ,
Why Me , why me every incident.

Why me all the time, why history to be cyclic to me,
It is fate targeting me, it is destiny want me,
For real am a statue, am left to wonder why me,
Everyone l see next to me, can not be with me,
Why everyone leaving me, am soon going to find me.
Why Me , why me every incident.
Recall well soon, less than anos,
I traced amigo , we vibe juntos,
Today am alone, why me each scene,
Why am l example , for many only me,
Can anyone , be used instead of me,
Am tired am tired, l wanna enjoy,
Just like others , juntos con mi amigos.
Why Me , why me every incident.
Why me every scene, maybe fate want it who knows,
No l wanna life like others, l wanna share with others,

However irony keep, repeating it self,
What mistake l deed , to suffer like this ,
Am l only person who , goes through this series,
I wanna know , looking my nature am holy as holy ghost,
Simplicity is my style , my way of living ,
Why Me , why me every incident.
Composed by: Tibez Albershile

73. Amor

"Amor"
I have found , a treasure ,
I have found , a heart ,
What l gonna say, l have found Amor,
Tell me anything , tell me about love,
Simple as a b c , can not wait to tell,
My amigos , l have found heart,
My Amor for life .
Simplicity is her nature, so stunning,
Yet humbled to all, can not imagine,
I have a Skylark , sunshine just like others,
I wanna be with mi Amor, next to her,
Listening to melody of her, enjoying good music,
Such are what am foreshadowing, with my Amor,
My Amor for life .
I see her as new , new creature,
New being that , Sir Jah created,
To give me company, when am lonely,
When am bored, to make me happy,
Can not compare, the love l receive ,
The love l read in poems, indeed she has over taken everything,
I see granting, her mi keys and password,
For mi heart and soul,
No one like her and no one to be like her , in my heart
My Amor for life .

Created by : Alberto Kelly

74. Am Busy

" Am busy"
Mi amigos , mi Amor,
What l gonna say , what l gonna do,
Stiii am bee , still occupado,
Poetry writing, wiii it give me time ,
Mi Moonlight , am sorry what to do,
Am busy Beebe, am busy moonlight.
Best days are coming, fast than deer,
Sun gonna shine, to mi sunshine,
Dark days gonna flew, away by her beauty,
The rain gonna hear , the cry of mi Amor,
Then mi hands , gonna be heavy,
To write to grant me , chance to see Amor,
Am busy Beebe, am busy moonlight.
Mi amigos , trust mi words y believe me,
One day in time, one day for a while,
Your poet gonna be free, free from writing,
Your fellow migo , gonna be with you,
Only matter of time, be optimistic Kelly gonna be free,
Free from writing , free from poetry,
Am busy Beebe, am busy moonlight,
When they see me, they ignore me,
They have created a barrier, just for Kelly,
They have turned away, away from Kelly,
Due to mi nature , mi lifestyle,
No man , no living thing,
Gonna create, gonna determine self destiny,
The more l try, the more l found,
Myself in a trap, that made by fate writing poetry,
Am busy Beebe, am busy moonlight,

Soon l gonna be through, mi Amor y mi amigos,
Soon you gonna get, your Amor,
Soon you will see, your sunshine ,
Soon you gonna sing, to your Skylark favorite santuri,
Soon you gonna disfruta, con Amor,
Soon all the wait, all the wept gonna be over,
Soon the faces, for Migos gonna shine like sun,
Soon mother gonna rejoice, to see the return of son,
Soon the long project, of Kelly gonna be done,
Am busy Beebe, am busy moonlight,
Composed by : Mad Poetic Editor

75. The food

"The food "
What to say, what to tell ?,
The same food, the great food,
That everyone was looking, was expecting to have it,
Even you had same dream, the food,
What happened to the food?
The glitter food, the same food,
Food that led to fight , the same food,
Food that was well prepared, the same food,
Food that was meant, for you the same food,
The food that was on your own hands, the same food,
What happened to the food?
The sweetness of the food, can not imagine the food,
The aroma of the food, that made men to seat and eat ugali,
From miles, provided their stomach gonna be full,
The food many were denied, you handed same food honorably,
Same food you can not , say a word today ,
What happened to the food?
Not even , the smell of it,
Not even, the taste of it,
Not even , looking what is made of,
Not even , putting hands on it,
Not even, thinking having it
What happened to the food?
Composed by: Map Poetic Editor

76. Mi last prayer

"Mi last prayer "
Thanks to Sir Jah, Thanks to Sir Jah,
What l gonna say, what l gonna ask ? ,
Many wishes y many desires , l have asked,
You have still fulfilled , for real am satisfied,
Mi last prayer , mi last prayer.
The last prayer , tiii end of time,
The last prayer, for poetry y poets,
The divine source, Sir Jah to give,
The poets the message, to light world,
The poets to deriver, Sir Jah message,
Across the globe , tii end of time,
Mi last prayer , mi last prayer.
Mi humble request , for the nation y world,
May the God the giver , for all to bring good,
Leaders to guide , the people towards the right path ,
To grant world , peace and harmony ,
To see prosperity for all , the nations,
Mi last prayer , mi last prayer.
Mi favourito Padre , Mi Giver y Saviour,
Mi last prayer , mi last prayer en last minute,
Mi last voice to say , to speak it ,
Mi amigos y familia members ,
All en mi prayer, to be en your hands,
To grant them , con peace y health,
Mi last prayer , mi last prayer.
The school y institution, are important ,
They are Pilars , to transform knowledge ,
Mi last seconds , tii my downfall,
All the education institutions, to be led by your light,

You to choose , good leaders to led ,
Your chosen race, to success of tomorrow,
Mi last prayer , mi last prayer.

It is now mi count down, para mi last seconds,
Thanks to Sir Jah, Thanks to Sir Jah,
For l believe , l trust you gonna,
Hear mi cry , you gonna hear mi prayer,
Mi entire prayer, prayer for all ,
To mi God , l believe everything ,
Gonna go bien, l know l trust that,
Amen
Mi last prayer , mi last prayer.

Composed by: Albert Nyangaresi

77. Kenya

"Kenya"
Thanks to Sir Jah, for real it is to his,
Grace we see we gut Kenya, for real we need to do something,
Why not to stop it , silly demonstration ,
We waste our own resources, why to demage ,
To ruin our nation, nation that our fore father's struggle ,
To fight for independence, for real it is painful,
Kenya my home, Kenyan lets build it.
It is awesome to follow , follow Constitution ,
To do demonstration , a peaceful demonstration,
We express our voice , after express the voice ,
We as good citizens , we but a side silly,
Roaming in towns ,
Go rurals to see , where you can fit y build the nation,
Nation is built by we, we build by working,
Kenya my home, Kenyan lets build it.
Why to kill even our brothers, men in blue ,
We have a role to do, to safeguard the citizens,
To sorry to narrate , to mother's the son,
The daughters they raised, raised of hardship,
Gone for eternity , the investment each,
Family member , done so painful ,
Kenya my home, Kenyan lets build it.
Let put a side , the fake influence ,
The fake people , whom wanna ,
Wanna see our nation , nation to pieces,
Let's we the leaders both , parties the opposition ,
The government , to talk with the Gen Z,
The country needs , the president as a father,
Father to be example, example for many ,

Kenya my home, Kenyan lets build it.
The new generation , the Gen Z are good,
The good to see , see the where the country ,
The Republic is going , let's give the government,
Time to address the issue, the president ,
The president is the head, he has to heart,
He is a father to nation, father to the family,
Let us give time, time for all issues ,
Issues to be addressed, peace for all,
Kenya my home, Kenyan lets build it.
Composed by:Alberto Kelly

78. Freedom fight

"Freedom fight "
Who gonna save us ?,
We need to be held, our cry for this nation,
Did we choose leaders or pigs?, why now all this?,
Why our cry , our pain are not held ?,
Our own government, standing against it's own citizens,
Who gonna save us ?,
Tears down the cheek, men in blue ,
On a hot sunny day , the blue sky,
Stand up raise , the guns to the same,
People that pay them, painful to say,
The fully armed , to face their own ,
Citizens that were , to protect as per Constitution,
Who gonna save us ?
So sorry indeed , so mercifully for Kenyan,
To who stand , stii to oppose the impunitive,
Biil that wiii make , the lives of Kenyan to be like hell,
When they raise voices, they are shot ,
What we gonna do , whom to tell for real?,
Who gonna save us ?
The future we are building, what a generation,
What we gonna say, kenya for real ,
Freedom press , free from expressing,
Fighting for their own view, no one is listening to,
The government , going against it own people,
It is a complex satution, it is granite indeed,
Who gonna save us ?
Composed by :Mad Poetic Editor

79. Gen Z

"Gen Z"
Today we can say it, why after all,
Tell them the heavy tax,
Tell them the in justice ,
Tell them the corruption ,
Today we gonna shout , shout to world,
To hear out our pain , to come to help us ,
Gen Z to fight , a rightful fight.
Good in appearance , good in talks,
Forgetting Gen Z , can not see ,
The false promises , we are tired ! ,
Do we have a constitution ?,
Do we have , the freedom ? ,
We really need to know , for this is too much,
Gen Z to fight , a rightful fight.
The power , given by people,
Why misuses the power ?,
The people casted , vote to you ,
You turn against them,
Calling your citizens , criminals , terrorists ,
Whom gonna call, the likes of Mzee Jomo Kenyatta,
To see this , are we free or slave of our own constitution? ,
Gen Z to fight , a rightful fight.
Days are always numbers, no one can change fate,
God grant knowledge , to whom that listen to him,
Why dictatorship , you wanna be Lacuna Kasoo ,
Maybe Majoka if , Lacuna can not fit,
People can not do peaceful , demonstration ? ,
Why the dirty hands , given a chance to determine rules,
Gen Z to fight , a rightful fight.

Souls are shot , on a hot sunny summer season,
Standing to exercise sovereignty , power that people,
Are granted so painful , no one cares ,
The Lacuna see, the terrorism act ,
Why Kenyan to suffer,
Why the constitution powers , misuse why for real?,
Gen Z to fight , a rightful fight.
The truth is painful, painful than death,
Yet we see view , wanna follow the path,
Why people to vote , vote for pig,
The pig to Majoka, worship money,
Forgetting people , background you are from,
This is a security treat, let's deal it with any way,
Meaning citizens , to be buried by their own leaders,
We gonna use KDF, just for citizens con water and posts,
Tears down the cheek, why now ,
Gen Z to fight , a rightful fight.
Better to call them , judas betrayals,
See individual benefits, may Sir Jah ,
See the Gen Z , whom fighting for freedom,
Fighting against their , own government ,
Maybe to follow orders , order to hell,
Orders to kill , killi innocent citizens,
Such crime are not seen, are encouraged why after all,
Gen Z to fight , a rightful fight.
Composed by:Mad Poetic Editor

80. Sad story to tell

" Sad story to tell"
Thanks to Sir Jah, for gift for life,
Life gift for , everyone not just ,
The rich or one with power, both the classes,
Get chance to , enjoy the free life ,
Then why to make some , people life to be exile,
The act or rape , rape since ages .
Why not to change , change even once like chameleon,
With the colors con , different backgrounds,
High time to end it , once for all the rape case in 21 century for good,
So sad story to tell.
Maturity is respect, maturity is doing things rightful manner,
Way to act to cocks, and chickens ,
They know no , mother nor sister,
Why to tarnish , to ruin people's lives,
Tears flow down the cheek ,
The act of rape , mature man with ,
Con five effective , co operating ,
Why to tell , for real it is a bad act rape.,
Why to conduct it , why not to condemn ,
Such vices in our society, say no to rape,
So sad story to tell.
Not only men do rape, even women do the act,
Imagine the women , that are seen as builders for the nation,
Build's of good family, con good moral values ,
Hoy raping their son's ? , where are we heading to ? ,
Why to make people feel, to die while young ,
Let's say no to such act, let's see mother's ,
Back to the right path ,for better tomorrow ,
So sad story to tell.

Rape is serious case, case that needs to be condemned ,
Both church , both political parties in rallies,
Or did the church leaders , the likes of Simon Peter ,
Died no one can stand, political leaders ,
Like of Kenyatta died , no more leaders to stand to say no to rape,
Maybe our courts , eyes are blind can not see the act,
High time everyone , everybody to stand firmly as affirmative to say no
to rape,
So sad story to tell.
All are not seeing , the society is going toxic,
The teenage are being ruined, young of age,
Let's the community , elders be elders for once ,
Let's bring the community , the society to rightful path,
Let's stand once and say no to rape, built the community ,
Con values and moral behaviors tiii end of time,
So sad story to tell.
Composed by:Albert Nyangaresi

81.Skylark for life

Title of the poem : -—"Skylark for life "
Gut one for life , Skylark ,
The simplicity is style , for mi Skylark,
Is the nature de, Skylark ,
Short cute y stunning ,
Melodies y moments,
She is mi heart , heart for life
Mi Skylark , mi Skylark for life.
Sweet melodic sounds , the voices,
Gonna make me , me to laugh y love,
Love her , mi Skylark for life,
Sunshine shine for her, to make her ,
To be more bonito , tii the end of time,
Mi Skylark , mi Amor what l gonna give ,
All mi regalos , all mi prizo l see,
Priceless mi Skylark,
Mi Skylark , mi Skylark for life.
Mi every second , mi minutes ,
I wanna seat , seat next contigo mi Skylark,
To share mi last , micro seconds ,
En mi Skylark arms , sleeping slowly,
Tiii eternity mi Skylark , mi sunshine,
I wanna love , l wanna share mi Encanta,
Only to mi Amor , mi Skylark .
Mi Skylark , mi Skylark for life.
The echoes of earth , your nombre,
Gonna be written , written en mi heart,
You gonna be known , know by all,
Know by love , the love,
Love of Romeo and Juliet, en the cyclic century ,

Only mi Skylark , not anymore of the others,
Mi Skylark , mi Skylark for life.

Composed by: Alberto Kelly

82. Tiii top

Tii top
Many things to be , done Migos,
Tii top mi Amor, Kelly needs,
To struggle , to suck libros,
Collaborative poems, contigo global
Poets the likes, de jabir from Niger,
Tiii top , tiii top Kelly.
To go globe , to be global poet,
Many things must , be put in place,
Simplicity should , be your nature,
Good example , example to many,
Humble to , do many collaboration ,
End error of poetry, poetry de money,
Tiii top , tiii top Kelly.
No man can , win win the race,
No one can be top, top without ayuda,
Kelly needs, help no man on his own island,
Call Kelly number one, number come with efforts,
Efforts are built , effort are created hoy,
Tiii top , tiii top Kelly.
Challenges for poets, they are basis,
Determiners the potential , the ability for a poet,
Tiii top challenges , competitions are must,
No one can gurge, the individual ability ,
With the bear eyes, just poems needed to be dropped,
Tiii top , tiii top Kelly.
It is cheap as a b c, how many are top?,
It all about self sacrifice, self dedication,
To be at top Kelly, Sir Jah needs ,
To be your friend, best friend ,

Friend for life , for all good things ,
The source , is Sir Jah no doubt to that ,
Tiii top , tiii top Kelly.

composed by: Mad Poetic Editor

83.Tears mixed with feelings

Tears mixed with feelings
What does it feel like ?,
Caring for someone who never cared about you.
What does it feel like ?
To be betrayed by someone you love most.
Would you be able to hold back your tears,
For real it is granite , no man can feel it,
The betrayal de Encanta, betrayal .
If a tear drop could, contain 1% of water and 99% of feelings,
How many percent of feelings would you lose if you cried all day ?
Casting away your feelings like a piece of trash
Throwing you into an emotional trauma.,
Will you be able to recover from it ?,
Will you be able to face your real self ?,
All long awaited hope crashed in a twinkle of an eye .
The betrayal de Encanta, betrayal .
The betrayal of love , is cutting across,
Not even poets , save from love,
The tears down cheek, gonna go one day,
The promises for poets, the loyal promises,
Sky is limited space is , our destination ,
We gonna be one , tiii eternity only we gonna ,
Be separated by fate, by a bad fate dead,
The betrayal de Encanta, betrayal .
Where did betrayal start ?,
Maybe the back days en , errors de Adam and Eve,
No one knew the betrayal , the betrayal is so headache,
The one that you see, loyal to sand of sea,
Better to cool mind, freeze mi heart ,
De Encanta for real , it is complex for all Skylark ,

The betrayal de Encanta, betrayal .
Betrayal !!!

84.Be mine forever

"Be Mine Forever"
Be mine forever, my love, my heart
Be mine forever, we'll never be apart
In your eyes, my soul finds a home
With you, I am never alone
Your touch ignites a burning flame
Melting my fears, soothing my pain
Your love is a shelter from life's storm
With you, my heart beats forever warm
Be mine forever , tiii the end of time,
Mi sunshine , mi Amor ,
Gut only you for life , l see you as regalo,
Sir Jah granted , to me mi Amor.,
Be mine forever, my love, my friend
Together our love will never end
Through laughter and tears, we'll stand as one
Forever entwined, our love will have won
© Al-Qordoweey © Alberto Kelly

85. Love to soak up

Love to soak up
Not hide a multitude of sins,
Let show a gratitude of sights,
even if, a sight for sore eyes,
let's your words,soak up the sun,
She lost her hearts on me,
She can't live without me,
She speaks, she freaks,
She spangles, she sparks,
Then, the sparkle of the diamonds,
The bright of the silver than storms,
The light of the stars than sounds,
She's gentle, calm, flamboyance,
She speaks like a billion hulks,
She looks like a million bucks,
Buck up, come on, nils aren't that bad,
The buck stops with; then here,
The buck of her ideas up; be there,
Never shut up, buck up, stand up,
Never pick up, to spare up, up up,
Goes on, lean on, come on, on on.
Written by: Jabir Mustapha
Country: Nigeria◇◇◇◇◇◇◇
my tribe: Hausa
Date: 16/5/2024.

86.Inspire on

Name: Jabir Mustapha
Country: Nigeria◇◇◇◇◇◇
5/July/2924

inspire on
Throw head away,
Toss yourself out,
Toss yourself on,
Bear yourself on,
Lean yourself on,
Lead yourself on,
Patience is possible,
Patience is power,
Patience is knowledge,
Patience is genius,
Patience is just like weapon,
Patience is as axe as success,
Success is as fruit as patience,
Sometimes is as restive as light.

87 . Broken heart

" Broken heart"
When l saw her , you know what?,
I felt for her, for real she was mi first ,
Skylark l had traced , en escula,
I thought her heart , gonna bite bit by bit.,
My first love was funny, like fuckies ,
I saw her and love her , forgetting love es feelings,
Both parties , the like of Romeo and Juliet,
I thought we gonna , be far like the sun.,
Time granted me, the best lesson,
Best way for real, to tell the broken,
Heart the heart , was hurt,
Hurt en nombre de Encanta,
Glitter es gold , for real ?,
Who knew simple as a b c, things gonna turn ,
The love story , gonna flew away ,
The way birds flew away, who knew ?,

Composed by Alberto Kelly

88. I Wii be your soldier

Theme: I'll be your soldier
" I Wiii be your soldier"
Mi promise to mi love ,come rain o sun ,
I gonna be next to you mi love,
I gonna be your soldier , my soulmate,
My heart , gut you for eternity.,
Life is complex , my Skylark ,
Believe me l gonna be , next to you,
Just as president y bodyguard,
Gut nothing to fear, am your soldier.,
My moonlight , fear nobody future ,
We are creating, continue be loyal,
I will be yours, for lifetime,
Your soldier , tiii end of time my love.,
Every single breathe, my love for you,
Am you my Skylark, you are me mi love,
Am ready to guide , mid night mi casa,
To see my love , enjoying the night.,
Composed by© Alberto Kelly
Country Kenya ◈◈ ◈◈

89. It's your turn

"IT'S YOUR TURN"
Your time has come, don't be afraid
To shine so bright, to show your shade
The world needs you, your voice, your might
To make a change, to shine with all your light
You are the future, the hope, the guide
Don't let fear hold you back, step aside
Take the stage, speak up, be bold
Your dreams are waiting, your story to be told
You have the power, the strength, the grace
To make a difference, to leave your mark on this place
So rise up, stand tall, don't give up the fight
You got this, you're ready, IT'S YOUR TURN to shine so bright!
And when the road gets tough, and the journey's long
Remember why you started, and keep moving strong
Draw on your courage, your heart, and your soul
You'll rise above the noise, and reach your highest goal◈

90. Be the way you are

"BE THE WAY YOU ARE "
written by sage poetry MW◇◇
In the land of the young and free,
Bright minds with dreams yet to be,
Embrace your quirks and talents glee,
And let your spirit soar wild and carefree.
Be yourself, stand tall and grand,
In a world where you take your stand,
Unleash your passion, let it expand,
And in your heart, greatness you'll command.
Believe in yourself, don't hesitate,
Your dreams are the compass that navigates,
The future is yours, don't procrastinate,
Embrace who you are, celebrate.
So wear your crown, let your light shine bright,
The world awaits the wonders you ignite,
Be yourself, pure and true in sight,
And in your authenticity, greatness takes flight.

91. Life and dreams

"Life and dreams "
Thanks to my God who,
Knows everything my keys,
Are always on his hands ,
He brought me gifts of,
Kelcys and Kante whom ,
Lit little light toward my ,
Dreams dreams of all,
Time poet the poet .
Many have come to ,
Challenge me challenge ,
It's self let them to tears,
To flew away sooner ,
Near future l see being ,
Written on books not written ,
Also known as great poet ,
For all time not this century ,
Also the golden gone time,
I gonna go there and do ,
Many more impressive ,
Work it's indeed amazing ,
Time poet the poet .
God is to grant us the gifts ,
That gonna make us go ,
Far to be stable and firm ,
To our society our role ,
It's to identify them to ,
Benefit from gifts for,
Indeed poetry is life de Kelly ,
Without poetry Kelly is nothing ,

What amazing poetry for life ,
Time poet the poet .
From first day Liz lit me ,
I saw my dreams high,
To be written in books ,
Not ending to bars for,
Tinny issues not at all,
To be light to led society ,
Seeking peace hide piece ,
What a dream to go,
Global to be inspire ,
To many so to be ,
Know of merits ,
Key to success to many,
Time poet the poet .
Composed by: Alberto Kelcys

92. Never give up

"Never give up "
Believe, trust on system,
You gonna be there , no matter how long,
The journey is full of ups, downs are obviously ,
Keep the spirit high , for one day you gonna be there,
Where many are, you gonna write a story,
Success story , surprise to many,
Never give up, never give up.
Satution can be a rock, leave with it,
See the hard time, build the hardness ,
Make yourself stronger, to see tomorrow,
Pulling up , surrendering is a phrase,
Phrase for , the weak ,
You were born , a fighter fight for your tomorrow,
Never give up, never give up.
Make them feel , feel you are there,
Do not act foolish , stupid to see,
Little success , to surrender,
Make the universe , to unite to congratulate,
To award you for , you have done it ,
You have set a settings , a base to be followed,
Never give up, never give up.
You wanna go , go globe ? ,
Then efforts , commitment ,
Needed to be put , put in place,
To see you top, to see you ,
In international television, telenovela products,
To see queen writer , Jabir the poet from Nigeria,
The other poets , outside Africa , inside Africa know you,
Never give up, never give up.

Not to poets , also to globe,
To good readers, to realize ,
To be affirmative , towards their goals,
To be committed , tiii five fit down the soil,
Never give up, suck knowdgle ,find the key to success,
Giving up is not , not style for many,
Style for few , few who see no future,
Born by women, raise by man ,
Never give up , never give up .
Composed by: Mad Poetic Editor

93. Pain of love

"Pain Love "
Snake bites, sweet than honey,
The love is love?, I wanna know,
Love is sharp than dagger
To all broken soul , gonna know ,
The sharp of the dagger, the one tasted,
Gone through pain of love, pain of betrayal,
Love created , love build,
Build in a environment , of trust honest,
The love that is beyond sea, beyond the see of man,
The love of promises , mine for life ,
Mi queen , mi Amor tiii end of time,
Take look, the sweetness of love,
See how love is appealing, how is sugar to lick.
Love pain can not, heal with words,
Love hurt heart alot,
The wounds remain fresh, for the broken hearts,
The pain of love, cut the senses,
Senses to see, see right and wrong ,
Why many took, the worst path,
The path of destruction, path of revenge.
Love is not laugh anymore, the error is gone,
When love was paradise, where love was love,
When love was valued , the golden days ,
Many wishes to see them , hoy no time,
No minute you gonna , get them back,
What gone no, way no chance to see ,
The days back , back to line .
Composed by:Mad Poetic Editor

94. Mercy

"Mercy "
No more , am tired for real,
No man is perfect, only God,
Many things , many stories,
Yet l denied , mi promises ,
All l broke them ,
For real am sorry,
Only l wanna , seek mercy,
Just mercy , mercy nothing more.
Mi pride made me, to be fool,
I did not see love, l see signs ,
Sighs of betrayal , yet you were ,
Loyal to sand of sea,
Why my eyes were not able to see,
Mi Skylark, mi Amor ,
You complete me , for life
Finding like you is granite, replacing you,
Has turned to, cement for real ,
Just mercy , mercy nothing more.
Only Mercy is to God, but deeply,
Your heart your soul, l believe that ,
Your gonna get , a space for me,
Forgive me, l feel burden for real,
Heavy loaded , loaded by sins,
Only you mercy , mercy gonna
Relief me , just mercy .
Just mercy , mercy nothing more.
Too like anyone , anybody l wanna ,
See paradise , l wanna be white ,
White to snow , l wanna feel free,

Free man when , l gonna receive ,
Your mercy , deeply l believe that,
Your true love, gonna fed away,
Your love is paramount, for eternity for you l see tomorrow,
Just mercy , mercy nothing more.
Bible stories we , learn forgiveness and repentance,
Why not to put in reality?, l am optimistic,
You gonna forgive me, l gonna get your forgiveness,
My heart , is waiting to see your mercy,
My face waiting , to face you dear one,
Time has given me tips, my pride is gone,
Am a new person, am a Christian am waiting,
To see your mercy , to see bound once again,
Just mercy , mercy nothing more.
Composed by Mad Poetic Editor

95. Panel of judges

"panel of judges "
Poetry! Poetry !, they call themselves,
The panel de poetry, panel to set rules,
Rules for all, forgetting themselves,
They see themselves, God for poetry,
So sorry , sorry for all poets,
Where we gonna ,go fellow Migos,
When we set rules , rules for others,
Who made us rules, who made us to see us righteous,
Who made us judges de poetry?, am a wondering jew ,
On a hot summer , when winter gonna shift ,
As fast as lightning , only preguntas.,
Let's be judges , judges for all,
Not for chosen race,
For chosen gender , poetry es big ,
No one can understand , poetry alone ,
As you see the panel , calling themselves,
The panel de elites , can't imagine,
Even think little de panel,
The silly panel , better to be erased .
Created by © Joker

96. Dialogue

"Dialogue "
Oooooh daughters , daughter of man,
Change before , changes change you,
Humble before , mighty before God,
You gonna see future ,.

Servant of God, Padre de church,
What to do hoy ?, tell us how to see,
See the risen Christ , oooooh servant,
The chosen one, guide us to God.,
Oooooh brothers , oooooh sisters,
Seek the way, way to repentance,
Ask forgiveness, forgive each other ,
You gonna see, eternity see paradise.,
Let's pray , let's humble ourselves ,
To the mighty God, believe trust ,
We gonna see paradise y God,
We pray all in Jesus , name amen ,

Composed by:© Albert Nyangaresi

97. Soon am leaving poetry

" Soon am leaving poetry"
Fast than lightning, not slow to tortoise,
Am going for real, am going from poetry,
Maybe am tired , of attacks ,
Am going l do not, need anyone any permission,
Am going far from poetry , am going to enjoy ,
Soon am leaving poetry, soon am leaving poetry.
Am tired of giving , giving best,
Some poets attacks, to simple ,
Too cheap language , am leaving poetry,
I hate for real , silly arguments ,
Am going to leave , the toxic poetry,
To rule the world, hopefully you ,
Gonna get ease, you gonna be relieved,
Soon am leaving poetry, soon am leaving poetry.
Am sorry to mi fan base, mi amigos ,
Who see mi going , global for real,
Am so sorry to mi Amor, soon am leaving,
No more of mi poems, am going from poetry,
I know l was soon , taking over the legends ,
Particularly to Poetry, to go miles ,
To sorry for mi fan base , across the globe ,
I had built mi big name, big bland of daily poems,
Soon am leaving poetry, soon am leaving poetry.

I need no one advise , l need no one ayuda,
Am leaving poetry , am pulling up,
Am stopping being a poet, l wanna self freedom,

No more worries , no more stress,
You believe you gonna do, best than me ,
You gut mi blessings, am tired for real,
I want a break , a leave for decades,
I wonder what gonna happen, what wiii guide society,
Soon am leaving poetry, soon am leaving poetry.

It is adiós to all mi amigos , adiós to mi fan base,
I do not know l gonna be back, back to poetry,
If a day you miss mi poems, go to any platform ,
Go search poetry de Encanta, go ahead to read ,
For real it is a sad day , dull day for poetry,
Tears down cheek, can not change mi decision,
Am going hopefully you , gonna recall me ,
Soon am leaving poetry, soon am leaving poetry.

Composed by : Mad Poetic Editor

98.Mi queen

" Mi Queen"
Gut a queen,
Queen for life,
Mi queen to kid,
Around like kid,
Oooooh,
What l gonna say,
Mi lines are overwhelmed by her,
Mi queen , needs king,
King of hearts ,
Not king of Thebes , Oedipus,
Just simple , king y humble ,
One sky y stars, definitely knows,
Tell me , mi queen for life.
Soon am going , mad mi queen,
Tell me more loud, mi queen,
I wanna hear it,
I wanna mi queen,
Nobody else ,
I Wanna give , mi heart to ,
Mi queen for real,
No worries , no pain ,
I believe , gut queen ,
Queen of principles ,
Tell me , mi queen for life.
Mi queen , your king,
Wanna you,
Your spendthrift ,
Is waiting for you,
Your Skylark want you,

Wanna see the black chocolate,
The queen for life , no doubt,
Mi queen , mi wish ,
To see her , her alone,
Tell me , mi queen for life.
What to say mi queen,
Am nothing , am helpless,
Mi kingdom , wanna know,
The queen , queen for life,
Mi maids , are tired of waiting,
They wanna , offer services ,
Services to , mi queen ,
Mi queen , nature simplicity,
The style , gonna ,
Kill me , your king
Tell me , mi queen for life.
Mi final minutes ,
Mi memories ,
Mi precious time ,
Mi dinero ,
Mi password and keys ,
Mi heart y soul ,
I wanna ,
Grant mi queen ,
Just as simple ,
As a b c ,
Like a regalo ,
Tell me , mi queen for life.
Composed by: Mad Poetic Editor

99.School

"school"
Tell me , tell me ,
I wanna hear , l wanna know,
The school , the poetry school,
The good in attractive, good in appearance,
Fake adverts posts , what a school,
Do you know the school ?
School a center, center of secular values,
School a home , far from home ,
The same school, turning toxic,
What a school for real , just tell me ,
Waiting to hear, waiting to listen to
Do you know the school ?
Wow impressive , amazing in identifying,
Good appealing , simple guys ,
To play with as bubble gam, to sorry for escula,
Days are numbered, sky is the limit for us,
Believe me beneath sun, nothing is hidden ,
Do you know the school ?
Thanks to Sir Jah, that few have gone through,
Most gonna get , to know the school ,
What values do we impact , to society to others,
Fake promises for support, for real the school is impressive,
Do you know the school ?
To surprise to amazing, to see from school,
Less in number , number to Count ,
Yet ready to tarnish, the good name de escula ,
To serious to see, the inquisitive to funny ,
To discover nothing more, nothing gained from escula ,
Do you know the school ?

Composed by:Tibez Albershile

100. Golden days

"Golden days"
For real , for sure l regret ,
Do l really have , same brain,
Do l have the same, memories for real,
Do l have same body , build up with bones,
Only questions , that rise in my mind,
When l think little , of my dark days,
The golden days .
The time l wasted , why for real for,
The fake stories, so sweet yet,
Yet mi eyes were blind, blind to see,
See the reality , see the resolution ,
Why mi heart to be carried, so quickly,
So fast than lightning, so fast to deer,
The golden days.
When l think , little of the same ,
My eyes filled , with tears to sorry,
Sorry for myself , yet l knew from ,
From the experience, that l read ,
Read from poems, plays and many literature works,
What a scene to see , on the present days,
The golden days.
No one is save , nor on safer place,
He gonna say , he gonna tell people,
That nothing gonna , harm him born,
With man have to feel, feelings the love,
Now the love depends , the giver of love,
Surely the golden days, stiii fresh in mind,
Golden days.
Whom said , whom said ,

I wanna know the guy, l feel to know him,
Poet's do not have feelings, poets are broken,
I wanna know , the guy for real ,
No one can predict , nor for tell future ,
Poet's to got broken, get attack by love,
The golden days.
High time to say it, to express it,
Time to utilize ,the knowledge of it,
Time to be firm, more than fountains,
To be affirmative, to focus for tomorrow,
To use it is exposure , to be people ,
Not to cry again , to wipe tears across ,
Migos to work , juntos for tomorrow,
The golden days.
Composed: by Tibez Albershile

101.Never give up

"Never give up"
Joan mi Amor , maybe is fate ,
All my efforts l make, day in y out,
All goes in vain, yet of say light at end of tunnel,
Maybe it is myth , l keep in mind ,
For real satution, is granite to say,
Feel to say adiós , to the universe,
Never give up, never give up.
Tomorrow is there , for you need ,
To stand to be hard, to diamond,
To face satution, to see fate what ,
Up to believe trust, tomorrow is better,
To impressive to , to say however ,
Can not say it, for real it is to be firm,
Never give up, never give up.
The worst days , the moments ,
Can not be gone, by flash lighting,
The minutes , the moments today,
I feel to stay back , to let everything,
Just to surrender , to allow mind be ,
Free from stress , from the world,
Desires to seek , mi Father ,
Never give up, never give up.
Brother why to pull up, why to give up,
Brother not you , everyone needs you,
Believe mi brother , trust we gonna be,
Where some are, we gonna be there ,
It is matter of time , you just trust the ,
Entire process to see, the tomorrow ,
Never give up, never give up.

Why to surrender mi child, to young for it,
You are future , you are generation to come,
Gather yourself mi child, do not allow worries,
To overdo you mi child, believe you gonna make it,
Make yourself proud of you , tomorrow needs you,
Never give up, never give up.
Composed by : Tibez Albershile

102. Moonlight

"Moonlight"
Why all this why
You are my heart
My only one no other
The universe us
Told to everyone this
I really see you in me
No more of cheeks
In our journey joan
Take me to your ecosystem
I obtain nutrients
From grass to graze
You wiii remain in my heart
Am tired of games of words
You have known me in months
Now from months to years
I wanna you be my love
Many good in eyes
But you are my sunshine
See every of my minutes
I wish to spend with you
Fear the cunning
Of this century
You are my la novia
I don't and won't listen
To the fake stories of them
My heart already is taken
Maybe l deed a mistake
But l believe no mistake l deed
Your love joan is just

Amazing no one can be like
My Skylark joan just imagine
How was anos from start

Mi dating you
Indeed was a joke
But what happened
My heart was kept
So secure place even
I wonder why all
When did l love her
Surely you are my
World no more stories
I really love you
My favourito one Joan
Just wait and watch
Our story going global
From first day dating
You l felt eternity
In our love in my life
No girl l ever date
Felt so bonding
Let them say
Everything yet
Year come and go
My heart in your hands
I don't worry let them wonder
My sunshine l indeed owe you
Million of things and yet to come
Cut me with your love slow by slow
Let me earn title in the society of your

Love my love
Composed by Tibez Albershile

103. My life in exile

" My life in exile"
What scene to see ,
See the true sad ,
Chameleon colors ,
Cant believe nor thought ,
Call brother , a brother ,
Call liar a liar no more,
Tired of this games ,
Judge just same way ,
You may desire to be ,
Treated Tibez,
Mi life in exile .
New day new la novia,
New cheek new face,
New story can't say ,
It but too much of ,
Something es extremely ,
Cansado can you feel,
The pain one goes through ,
Seeing a brother playing ,
Games de kids cant imagine ,
My lifestyle my rules ,
Impresses no body ,
My life in exile.
Impress her so much,
Make her feel deep down,
She has found a caring ,
Hombre forget humble ,
Background that you came,
From what stupidity what ,

Mentality in mind tears ,
Down cheek watching just ,
Like a spectator ion cant do,
Anything nor anymore of,
Advice to mi amigos ,
Mi life in exile.
Time is best solution ,
Cant wait tiii right reloj,
So stunning so ready ,
To search so sucking,
Dinero machine what ,
Agony what state to ,
Whom to elaborate ,
The statement so ,
You gonna get mi ,
Amigos cual esta ,
Hablamous only ,
Speculation en mind,
My life in exile.
Composed by Tibez Albershile

104. mixed language

" Mixed language"
World is wide with variety
Of languages , start with English,
One of the most , popular global,
Language for the world,wow it's
Amazing to hear , the sane statement,
Buenos Dias , to Espanola to English
Just morning , just world full of
Wonders it's language variety,
Mixed language, Mixed language.
The same boy ,we call in English,
So surprising, to Espanol its El Niño,
Who thought , nor expected to.hear,
Such phrases, in deed day world,
The languages , do share real bond,
That's is a proof of Espanol and French,
In that some word are like similar,
The word man , in English to Espanol,
It's hombre , to French it's Homme,
Mixed language, Mixed language.

Maybe this languages, might have ,
Common ancestor , who knows
For this are , European languages
That's why have bond , from English ,
To French to Espanol, not word alone
Also the sentence , building the vocabulary,
The world indeed it's a mixture , of languages who knows,

That world it's has many languages
It's all about exploration,
Mixed language, Mixed language.

Walk nations , walk across the globe
Even learn the greetings alone, know buenas nouches , means good
night,
In Espanol discover ,disfruta means enjoy in Espanol,
For real exploration , across the world gonna improve not just
experience,
Also vocabulary, pronunciation and spelling for words,
This world it's a world class of language
We use language ,
Without knowing , the source, the background de language,
Just for communication, indeed we are human we wanna cheap things,
Mixed language, Mixed language.
Composed by : Mad poetic editor

105. White doves

" white doves"
What value , what treasure ,
The only one, true it's peace,
Time gone , many we fought,
The journey, the broken hearts,
However we have , healed up,
The time is for peace , for best of tomorrow,
Some see stupid are who, seeks peace,
Peace for life, peace for life.
Forgetting that for this , life peace is gift,
Why to worry, of conflicts just peace,
Peace makes impossible possible,
Find peace, find personality,
Search peace search, true meaning for success,
For peace is universe, universe is peace,
That is rule of nature, no one can alter, nor change it,
Peace for life, peace for life.
Nation fight , for individual beings
However the end of the day, found themselves,
Coming up for peace, people can not stay with peace,
Peace is element of nature, it's part of life,
For both man and everyone in earth, seek
Peace seek individual,
Prosperity in all levels, academic and the mental growth,
Peace for life, peace for life.
Composed by: Alberto Kelly

106.Should l share.

"Should l share"
My morning star , my sunshine,
Am in a dilemma, day in et out,
Your love, l see it's beyond measure,
Your sweetness, gonna finish me,
Am a statue mi star, l feel universe,
Gonna need, to feel it, to taste it,
They believe no , no more Encanta,
Should l share.
People see am , your slave can we,
Let them feel , the same bond mi bone,
It's time people, gonna know am you,
You are me mi Amor, no worries,
Fear less by bird, since l only got you,
Over million only one , name rungs in ,
Mi mind, the sunshine , the morning star,
That l made covalent bond , for life no other one,
Should l share.
Tears down the cheek, doesn't go in hand,
The beauty the smile, can not imagine tears,
Sorry for mi Amor, caring it's sharing,
Mi Amor l know , you fear the cute stunning,
Gonna capture me , capture re capture and flew away,
No mi Amor, just l wanna them see ,
True love , feel feeling of love only that,
Should l share.
Preguntas en your mind , allow it to cool,
You now am book , you are the topics,
You are rain and am your sun, to maintain peace,
The ecosystem , wanna see it see everything,

Towards the right , position the right path,
For prosperity, that why mi Amor l request we gonna do it,
For this simple, soul to know love,
Understand love , for love it's greatest gift,
That Sir Jah granted upon , us to use it to effective,
Should l share.
Composed by:Alberto Kelly

107. Once in a while

"once in a while"
For the dark face is winding up,
For the light is soon shining,
For a long time , for the endless hurts,
For once in a while, Kelly gonna be wiped,
The tears down the cheek, gonna get one true amor,
To be with him, that gonna make a new chapter,
For once in a while, all gonna be over,
That time is coming , for once in a while.
Those amigos whom flew away, for they gonna return,
The lost treasure, the lost lovers gonna return,
For the life of Kelly gonna , be in a new chapter,
New beginning , towards the best of tomorrow,
That moments that feelings, gonna be felt for once in a while,
That heart of longing to love , gonna get duplicate ,
That time is coming , for once in a while.
Time for new reigh , time for better world,
That people have been dreaming, have been foreshadowing,
That moment it is gonna be experienced, once for a while,
The end of suffering, the end of poverty ,
The end of heavy tax , soon they gonna be done ,
Only optimistic to be in people, the good leadership,
Good living standards , good families gonna be seen ,
Only once for a while , when everyone co operate ,
That time is coming , for once in a while.
The paradise we read in bible, the holy nation,
Our feet gonna step, on the same ground,
Our sins gonna be wiped away, our face gonna be new one,
Just we gonna be like Jesus, just once in a while,
The dream of seeing the sky , seeing our lord ,

That minute gonna be here , we need to be ready,
We need to prepare ourselves, for such a scene ,
The scene that comes , for once in a while ,
That time is coming , for once in a while.
All the pain on earth , all the suffering,
Gonna be gone , we gonna disfruta,
Those with or without, dinero what a scene,
We gonna be all in same terms, we gonna be feliz,
For once in a while we gonna , get true Encanta,
Nobody never nor thought , nobody knew such seen,
Everyone gonna taste , the love gonna feel the feelings,
The true friendship , once in a while all the tears gonna be gone,
That time is coming , for once in a while.
Composed by : Mad poetic editor

108. The broken hearts

" The broken hearts"
We say goodbye but really want them to stay
We die a little in those one hand waves
Eyes holding back oceans
Hearts slowing down motion
We tell ourselves ..we'll see them again
Tomorrow maybe ..
But not days far away
Or they'll change their minds
And come running into our arms
But they don't..
With the weight of souls that have never known distance...
We turn ...and leave...
And hope they have little reminders of us..
At a glance at stars...or a song we loved..
A path we walked. Or the jokes we made..
And the love within us turns into an angry serpent that bites and bites
..into itself ...
And we end up being poison ...
Dreading goodbyes..
And the skies ..and anything that could make us cry ...
Because a cry for a hurt toe could end up being a cry for a broken heart
...and being treated like trash...and not finding your shirt. And all the
emotions you bottled up finds way out...all thanks to the toe...
But deep deep down..
We hope...
They have little reminders of us...
Maybe then they'd halt...
And turn..
Composed by Shel

109.Echoes of hope

Echoes of hope
"A new era dawns, with tears in our eyes,
We search for true friends, but they're hard to find.
We roam, like madmen, chasing shadows and lies,
Afraid to open up, lest our lives be left behind.
Promises are empty words, worthless and untrue,
Disappointment reigns, a constant we can't renew.
Those around us seek to bring us down,
Deceit and lies, a twisted passion, a wearisome frown.
Only family cares, a rare solace we find,
No one to trust, no safe haven to unwind.
Growth and happiness are met with scorn and disdain,
A cruel world, where joy and sorrow are intertwined.
But still we must stand on our own two feet,
We have no one to help us but ourselves,
Treat others with kind,
Let's change the way we live, to make the World anew.
Composed by : By Azbee

110.I AM ME

"I AM ME"
"I'm me,
I'm pleased with my life as it is,
I'm helping others, doing my best in all things.
I'm not begging anyone for assistance,
Bravery is my fashion.
I'm taking responsibility for being good to others,
I'm not allowing anyone to hurt others.
I'm not going deep to see the life of others,
I'm focusing on my future.
I'm not disappointing anyone,
I'm telling the truth everywhere I find myself.
I'm behaving carefully, so I don't hurt anyone.
I'm always a virtuous person
I'm a human being, a fault-maker, but I always seek to apologize.
I'm not perfect, but I give my best.
Can you be like me?
So that our society will grow up with a better vision for the upcoming
young ones in the future."
Composed: By Azbee

111. In search

" In search "
On the way , on the way
To discover Encanta, on the way,
Hopefully l gonna, get best research,
Many have, entered have failed,
Many designs, many methods,
To trace love, many support needed,
In search, in search de Encanta.
The journey looks, granite in search,
I need help, to be successful ,
In search for Encanta, mi amigos,
What did l received , what did l found,
I saw it is one in a million, one in thousands,
No earth and tiil end of time, gonna get,
Such treasure, the treasure for life such,
Treasure such regalo, they are traced rare,
The treasure was Sophie, more than amigo,
More than Amor, indeed it is awesome,
In search, in search de Encanta.
The search needs time, search needs determination,
What a search there are many, good in eyes good in speech,
Too toxic in character , to sorry to say amor to such soul,
Nobody is safe , nor the upcoming generation,
The search it is tiresome, too complex to tell,
The search towards , Encanta the worst search in life,
In search, in search de Encanta.
All went in vain, the search for Encanta,
The material put in place, the dinero spent,
All went for granted , no one to tell,
No one wanna here, all meet in the journey,

Joke like Joker, just to hurt one heart,
What a search, to horrible search,
To sorry to audience, to hear the search,
That the sign were see, to be optimistic,
To end in tears the funny search, the search for love
In search, in search de Encanta.

Composed by Alberto Kelly

112.The end

"The end"
The end, de Encanta no , no cant believe,
It's the end that love, that feeling isn't there,
The one loved you, has find another heart,
The heart loved you , it's gone it's has been captured,
The one loved you alot, she is gone for good,
What a terrible end.
Man is to words , God is to amazing works every thing ,
Every drop of this earth, can't operate without him,
Cry for no reason, cry for lover whom has seen sugar,
To lick far end, the love story it's a riddle,
The riddle that, need one to think big,
What a terrible end.
The sweet , moments we shared together,
The memories of lovely , messages my love my sunshine,
Gonna they be swept away, wiii my heart be taken again by love,
Cant think even , l know meaning of love,
Only love of gift and fruit, of the holy spirit,
Not the love , love for tears
I don't think l know such love, better to trace the gift and fruit,
What a terrible end.
No one knows his or her destiny, no matter how powerful you are,
No one can change fate , regardless ,
Your money , your influence in the universe,
Everything belongs , to one name greatest of all God,
Cry for losing , God not losing lover,
Cry your day are up, yet you haven't asked for mercy,
Cry that no one , is there to led you
To righteous path,
Indeed gonna be the end, never shed tears for fake love,

What a terrible end.
Love is just like chameleon, changes with dynamic,
No one knows when , your lover gonna change,
No one knows , when the sweet love,
The beautiful moments, gonna be night mere ,
For the entire life, no one expects to be left so silly,
However has rule of nature, what has start must have the end,
Pray for better end, pray not to realize you are chasing leftovers,
Pray to avoid falling into temptation, temptations of forcing love,
What a terrible end.
Composed by:Mad poetic editor

113.Kelly the champion

" Kelly the Champion"
Call Kelly , number one,
The champion de Encanta ,
Done many Encanta pieces ,
Kelly the poet,
Everyone wanna my verse ,
Kelly the champion ,
Kelly master de Encanta ,
Kelly champion, Kelly champion.
Days have gone since l saw ,
A championship yet am champion,
Kelly have built a brand ,
On bare rocks ,no one knew ,
Kelly the error of the week it's over ,
The errors Kelly kept crying for,
Encanta has been gone, Kelly
The champion of hearts,
Kelly the master of lines ,
Kelly champion, Kelly champion.
What new to the champion,
What version, what tricks ,
You gonna fool Kelly with ,
Call Kelly ,the champion ,
Better not best Jah is best ,
All the time Kelly the poet ,
Has inspired many , has done many,
Not just poetry alone only ,
To this error, no one gonna see ,
And recognize Kelly efforts,
Kelly champion, Kelly champion.

Call Kelly championship by facts,
Call Kelly the champion of hearts ,
Both broken y the un broken ,
Kelly the champion , grant challenge ,
We gonna, compete on going ,
Global not silly challenge ,
Kelly the champion, simple soul ,
Simplicity es my style ,impressive
Cero stupidity, cero blues y greys,
Kelly champion, Kelly champion.

Composed by: Alberto Kelly

114Am on the away.

"Am on the way"
Mi Amor , mi Amor ,
Be patient trust me mi Amor,
Indeed it's a long journey,
However am still on the away
Stop asking , l left mi Amor,
Am on the way .
The long awaited soon gonna
Be over when we gonna unit
Mi amor it's all to wait for feedback,
When you gonna see me in your arms
The dark days , are passing away
It's time for two currents if different
Charges to fuse , am on the way
The journey it's tiresome not only you
But also your la novio , wanna see you,
Am on the away.
It's time to see the gifts ,
It's time to see mi Amor for decades ,
It's time to say hello to home,
It's time to seek blessings not , just
From mother but also father ,
It's time when l gonna go to light the society with values,
It's time to meet with friends for,
Long span of time ,
Am on the away.
The longing soon gonna be over ,
It's time it's now mi Amor ,
Mi favorito one to disfruta con me,
Reloj to see mi Amor , mi Amor

The time it's tending lowly, it's time
Now acting as barrier , it's time
We gonna meet , juntos con mi Amor,
The final , destination , gonna be ,
It gonna be on your arms
Am on the away.
Composed : by Mad Poetic Editor.

115.Your Day

" It's your Day"
Thanks to God
Thanks to parents
To reach this day
The day soul was
Brought to earth
Earth of wonders
It's your day carol.
Carol simple
Soul good friend
So dedicated to see
Smile on face of friends
What amazing scenes
Just lets say happy
Turning to carol
On of best friends
For life for Kelly
It's your day carol.
Day that each
Family member
Were waiting to
Welcome a soul
The day decoration
Were made to see
The little one carol
Smile for the long
Period , the endurance
It's your day carol
Vibe possible way
Keeping the values

Impress moral values
To your journey indeed
You gonna go far
Pray to Jah to grant peace
Of mind and soul
The key to success
They are on Jah hands
Do your best in all
Time rest leave to jah
It's your day carol.
Sunshine like star
Keep dreams high
The sky to see
How to attain them
Impress simplicity
However simplicity
Can't be changed
Since it's your nature
Sing to your day
Day like this soul
Was born the soul
Carol
It's your day carol.
Composed by Tibez Albershile

116. Migos

"Migos"
Tell me more and more,
It's interesante to hear,
Call friend from far,
To party for our dinero,
Am now full of pesos,
I wanna to work things,
So mi amigos gonna,
Feel paradise particular,
To this event of evening.
Call all the ladies,
You wanna have ,
All are for you ,
Remember to be careful,
On today actions for ,
The welfare of tomorrow,
Why to tell you ,
Yet you know,
It's because you,
Are mi amigos,
And that what amigos,
Do to fellow Migos.
Make more fun,
See the funny,
Girl from far,
She look so cute,
Amazing indeed,
Not all glitter is gold,
Yet she is my sunshine,
When wiii we reach to ,

Hear and l talk to her,
I feel to be feed,
By her love .
Migos Migos,
Esta dai esta dai,
Enjoy everything,
Feel yourself,
Maybe this is ,
Last chance on line,
So try to use to fullest,
Why memories more,
Daily basis do they,
Come to mind,
Am completely,
Hurt wiii day,
All be over melodies,
More touching.
Fake friends for real,
Forced made me,
To enter to a un wanted,
Universe to meet ,
My destruction to,
Touching to hear to,
Call friend call to ,
Satan to speak to,
Such liars day to ,
Today to our story.
Composed by Tibez Albershile

117 . The flower l bought

" The flower l bought"
When l gonna reach mi casa
When l gonna place mi
Nuevo flower
When l gonna show off mi
Flower to migos
Can't wait can't waste
Reloj l wanna disfruta
Con mi flower spend pesos
Dinero para mi flower
Watching every minute more
The flower l bought
I wanna nothing
I just want the flower
The delicate one
Finding it was granite
Hoy having it cant
Want anyone to kid
Just with mi flower
Even l don't want to
See the birds seeking
To sack scent it's
Just be mi only flower
The flower l bought
Minutes after minutes
Just ready to feel feliz
Indeed it's amazing
Even the appearing
Can't make you to
Go away from it just

Feeling to seat next to
Flower having peaceful
Moments more enthusiastic
The flower I bought
Composed by Alberto Kelly

118.The memories

"The Memories"
My ink to write, my ink to narrate the sweet,
Love story we shared, the infinite love at all,
The sweet moment we, spent as lovers so sweet,
To recall how love, was indeed sugar for all.,
Of ours how we enjoyed, the little games,
The beautiful places, we spent together only hoy,
Memories and melodies, who to say the story,
Who to hear me, my heart is hurt con the games.,
Recalling the sweet, melodic santuri es I turn mad,
The lovely touches, the kisses no at all,
I feel to trace between, the sky and land at all,
For soon am turning, to mad for memories.,
My good friends what, to say to you today,
My good los padre, gave me advice as son,
I heard them no at all,all was a waste or time,
See me today, my life is to Oedipus full of memories.,
Composed by Alberto Kelly
Country Kenya
Copyright © Alberto Kelly

119.Music festival

"Music festival "
A long wait day it's here ,
Day to dance to tunes,
Day to wear the warrior ,
Like form day is hear ,
The music festival.
Day we exchange ideas,
Day we learn more of,
Cultures can you know,
Maa is one of most ,
Favourito culture for,
The kenyans l gaze you ,
Have cero of information,
Let's dance to folk to ,
Abagusii culture ,
One of the golden,
Culture in decades,
The music festival.
Brother against brother,
Sister against sister,
What a day you can't,
Even think are same entity,
Yet from one mother wow,
It's passion of music music,
Let's dance to tunes de music,
A festive to be recalled for,
Years to come years to go,
First time to see such,
Simple heart for real ,
Music is to tunes even ,

Love tunes l gonna dance to.
Composed by Tibez Albershile

120. Home

"Home"
My home ,my hell on earth ,
Can't imagine nor think of,
Many more familiar y family ,
Wanna see mi gonna go,
Down to feet to polish their ,
Shoe cant imagine yet call ,
Home indeed it's hell,
Many feel paradise particular ,
When such moments arrive ,
The moments mother's meet,
Their children, complete of journey ,
The long tiresome journey coming ,
To climax indeed home is the best,
To me my home l see gonna be Maa,
So sorry to narrate my narrative ,
No one gonna hear it,
Home to be monitored , home to get ,
More painful ,psychological and mental ,
Can't imagine, the same home still ,
You wanna l go the house of conflict ,
The house of pieces for my peace ,
Maa is my home, to stay forever tiii,
My father decides my fate ,
Despite how far, from home it's better ,
Place to see and explore maa culture ,
Say to sorry ,and to lowly to home,
No more no more no, one is coming ,
No one is coming, l wanna peace,
I wanna study , l wanna study ,

I have chosen, academic and success,
Home is hell on earth ,
They say East and West home is best,
To me home is exile, Maa is my home .
Composed by Mad poetic editor

121 .The boy child

"The boy child"
Today tomorrow same story
Same boy child ,same time
We gonna want same boy
To inter mingle with our ladies
Tears to see such society
Where we bury our own
The boy child.
No one ready to side you everyday
Same boy being mentioned now
It's a song to some of us
Same government where such
Cases gonna go no help
Whom to a side with boy child
We are busy burying future generation
The boy child.
Such simple souls are wronged
Yet no one can stand to say it
The irony of it happens the
Story change same soul
Simple find himself again in sucks
Why all this why boy child
When Wii boy child voice
Wiii be recognised
The boy child.
Lost in drugs , lost in drugs trafficking
Lost in all crimes, can't imagine
Taking alcohol , to release stress
Same boy child , you see as son
Finally same boy , child ending

Up to bars even some , five fit down
Yet we can't see we are burying
Generation by our misconception
The boy child.
Composed by Tibez Albershile.

122. Freedom

"Freedom"
The all anos for battle
The age of dark error
Soon gonna be over
Our expectations are really
High the smiling faces
Indeed represent the same
Long journey soon gonna
Be over can't imagine
Free freedom.
The new reign gonna rule
The white colors are fading
So enthusiastic to see the Migos
From all sides are with us with
Any decision we gonna make
The feeling of free self guidance
The freedom from to land
Can't imagine nor think settlers
Mansion gonna be mine
The white Highlands gonna be
Ours again that is awesome
Free freedom.
Can't wait anymore just
Waiting for the hour to shout
We are free to run our on Republic
Our on nation emphasizing
Culture and traditions were cut off
By the West education cant wait
Anymore am more anxious to see
The handing over the power

Free freedom.
The fighters feel the value
De battle they fought with
The white the efforts gonna
Be know no more of slavery
The error of human trafficking
The error of white it's re solution
It's here the prophecy being fulfilled
The feeling of self ruling, self implementation
Indeed it's a jubilee that we waited
Anos being fulfilled
Free freedom.
Composed by Tibez Albershile

123. The hole

"The hole "
Good to go famous
Good to be known
Good your story to be
Told to everyone
Good that everyone
Gonna talk about you
The same hole.
The hole no one is safe
The safe are one who
Servers sir jah always
Away from dirty things
The one who seeks
The heavenly wealth
The servants de Jah
Cant imagine of few
In number however
Safe from satanic
Games as bubble gam
The same hole.
The rich the poor
Gonna find pesos
To spend to attain
The hole the hole
Has been since decades
Stiii sucking pesos
To our de day generation
The hole to pleasure
The hole of enjoyment
The same hole.

Heart created by jah
Desires , lust are nature
Of human why now
No one knows nor
Understand only jah
The giver ,the creator
The hole that has put
Many to five fit
The hole that brings
Generation to existence
The same hole that is
Played led to climax
The same hole.
Composed by Tibez Albershile

124.The one l hurt

"The one l hurt "
Deep down you are the
One l choose days
Weeks even months
Can't imagine day
Offline without texting
The one l love
The one l choose
I choose over many
Good in appealing
Good in goodbye
Can't believe you are one
Days have gone good
Deeds you deed
To Tibez stiii fresh
Can't imagine when
I gonna get a last
Chance to chase
You mi Amor l really
Regret mi little games
I played games now am
Watching the game with
The others can't believe
Time has given me good
Reason can't try
The little game babe
The one always chooses
Tibez all the time however
Can't imagine today
She isn't there one

Whom lit love to me
Whom thought me
Nature true colors
Of love not this love
Love for lust
But eternity love can
I forget all that fai
Can l forget for real
Two good anos with
You can't imagine
Can't believe
Composed by Tibez Albershile

125..GIFT YOUR ARE A GIFT

"GIFT YOUR ARE A GIFT"
Your gaze in the night
Brings me delight,
You touching me,
Is a blessing made,
You are a flower,
Brought from far,
You touch me,
I glow without fire,
A hot smile,
Always in time,
You the little one,
With more love,
A gift you are to me,
Always spending time,
Around you is the best gift,
That i deserve day and night,
With you around me,
I feel the true breeze,
We are the new lover birds,
Always together wishes,
Will come to be,
We will make it a blaze,
To the world it will light,
Love is our light,
It shows us the true path,
Following it me and you we are enough,
ROVY THEPOET MORE OF A POET
#champion booy is the smart guy we got
#KING' OF UNIVERSE POETRY

126. SHE BROUGHT ME BACK

"SHE BROUGHT ME BACK"
I left home away from mum,
But here I found my mum,
Who is and will still be,
My favorite care giver build of love,
She nurses me all time,
Am a baby once again this time,
I cry she makes me laugh,
Am down she smiles and i laugh,
This retrieves,
My happiness,
Finally am young again,
Going through the process again,
Slipping through her thighs,
Sucking her boobs,
Like I did years ago,
Like to mama I used to,
Am finally a little one I guess,
She is the empress,
She reminds me of my childhood,
When I played without any bad mood,
She cuddles me,
It is a song and poem at time,
Yesterday we sang together,
I so her smile awesomely clear,
When I got to her lower jaw,
I kissed it without any law,
I was undecided and low,
But this lead me championed like raw,
Am finally clear like a heaven law,

She is mine forever and that is a law
ROVY THEPOET MORE OF A POET
#champion booy is the smart guy we got
#ARENA KING OF UNIVERSE POETRY

127. True friend

"True friend"
Friend for life
No day no time
He can judge me
Either good or wrong
Mi favorito father
Mi best friend
For decades
Not just fake
Friends for no reason
The true friend.
Just satisfied seeing
Our friendship our bond
Child and father too
Enthusiastic to see
Can't pay anything
To appreciate the
Love the care l received
The true friendship
Can't be bought
With money can't be
Handled recklessly
Indeed the friend
I got cant afford to loss
Him the best all the
The true friend.
No place that l gonna
Go to hide from him
He is always next to
Me come good or bad

Side or any satution
My deeds aren't worth
Having true truthful
Friend like him
However he tolerate
Can't have such friend
In this century so
Caring each day smile
On my face
The true friend.
No day finger pointed
To me till today
No complains to me
Compared to cast
Friends de dinero
No peace , however piece
Yet can't see l really
Feel paradise to see
The state am let them
Stare as statue cant
Care provided
Got mi amigo con me
The true friend.
Composed by Tibez Albershile

128. True love

"The true love"
Can't find one like her fore real
Time has its own way of working
Indeed God is to deed
Man to work of hands
Can't believe but l believe
True love exists
Love is real not games
The true love.
Feel love by loved one
Never thought nor imagine
My text left Lopez to tears
I didn't know where to
Seek help after all
I deed l felt to drop tears
Down the cheek yet
You know men don't cry
She loved me yet l didn't
See she was ready to reply
Me any minute l typed
Yet l didn't see
The true love.
The love that can't be bought
The love that isn't shared
The love of eternity for
Real its true love not illusion
Never thought never imagined
That I was loved so deeply
Can have eyes yet eyes are blind
Can have ears however cant hear

The love from far forever
Can't nor imagine
I was now cousin to Thomas
The true love.
Love that l received l really
Think l gonna go anywhere
I feel for a while l found
A site to settle for ages
A heart to make a home
A love to be in love tiii end
If separation to send us path
That gonna be five fit down
The ground the love l see
For really l see paradise
Can't imagine it in this century
The true love.
Composed by Tibez Albershile

129. The return

" The return"
The heart was waiting a home
A home to settle for while time
Has gone yet the love felt from
The first day still is lit in mi heart
The return l feel little peace
I miss a lot cant manage to say
Yet l feel to speak and share
To mi heart mi Amor
Text made me away yet
Same text made me to
Hear from you same text
Gonna re light the lost love
Mi lovely Lopez can't wait
Just to see the bound
Built once again alone
Can't handle the task at hand
Need your support mi Amor
The return strike mi heart

I feel to thank mi God
The blessing l see each
Day make mi to humble myself
Each minute each second to say
Just a simple thanks to Sir Jah
The season the stories the destiny
Belong to him without forgetting fate
For man relay on the same hands

The gift received cant let it go
Gonna hold it carefully tiii
I see myself end of time with it
Search one like her is silly
Can't be found can't be traced
Having one like her it's a treasure
Can't be measured by coins
Just trust and loyalty pillar
Everything to be settled
Can't believe the return
The return that has impressed
Me the heart isn't hurt anymore
Just been captured capture re capture
Amazing scene to see on my face
The return .
Composed by Tibez Albershile.

130. The funny girl I meet

"The funny girl I meet"
Joke but not joker wow so amazing so,
Desperate to have a lover to be loved
What I got was more than love so funny
Cant imagine nor thought continues
My simplicity and the funny
La novia I have found for sure am
Finished the sky is seeing
the funny girl I meet.
Where did I trace such girl my life
Was sweet sugar to lick now see
My life is duplicate of hell in love
Just word love fake love cant believe
So annoying so stubborn sad story
No one is paying heed to nor elders
Nor even myself she see everything
Belong to her and her alone
The funny girl I meet .

I believed I had experience of love
Yet I see it's my new year my new
Style to love the sucking dinero
What a dramatists I interacted
With what state I brought to
Where is the way of the mad of her
Gonna make me more mad the stories
Of her are outstanding my mind
Can't believe cant imagine

The funny girl l meet .
The tall but not tall however flag post
The dark in nature yet not ready to
Agree she see herself white skin
Cant imagine the rudeness even can't
Be soot any society in our time no more
Talkative more of boring
Wonder what type of family society
She is the people l see as her amigos
Simplicity is seen clearly no doubt
The girl l meet .
Composed by Tibez Albershile

131. Mistake

"Mistake"
Maybe my mind is wrong
Why when l see my plans succeeding end up to worst
When will l see her my only loyal love
Or did l make a mistake making her my heart
Am left without any answer
My time my efforts l have to dedicate to my Amor
Nature grant me many million chances l can not blame it
Let me listen to my heart before my next step
My heart is attached to her so is my queen
I have to come with something like standard timetable
Since she is my only one and true love
Am compel to think beyond the box
Coming out with best plan since surrendering isn't my phrase
Tomorrow l need to think and think best solution
Actually Tiberius isn't know of failure
Tell me all you wish but not to fail
My amor time has challenged me
But never shake we are together tiii
Eternity let them say what they feel
You are my missing piece of my life
Your love from start tiii end l am statue
No one gonna be like you my love
Joan this journey is so complex
Yet your support l see success
No more of worries of anything
All mistake aren't it's nuevo anos
Means nuevo stories of Encanta
See mi la novia what they wanna
Do to blame me yet you are with me

So surprising my Skylark
Composed by© Tibez Albershile

132.Women de choice

" The Women de choice "
Sun high on the sky mi Amor
Cant Denny mi amor you
Have completely taken mi
Heart only mi heart can
Say it yet it just feel you
Alone and only one mi Amor
Let the universe see mi Amor
You are the one l have taken
Million stunning yet Sophie
Is the one only one
The one l choice.
Call me crazy de Encanta
Yet she has kept me calm
Miles and stories so enthusiastic
Ready to say to mi Amor Sophie
She can't Denny it she knew
She is only one and one
My choice from many
Who l have interacted contigo
Surely l have gotten a soul
To love me
The one l choice.
Call joke a joke but love
She has shifted en mi heart
Cant Denny that love doesn't
Exist indeed love is interesting
Cant waste this opportunity indeed
She has captured me capture
Re capture in her heart cant

Denny the fact just mi Amor
What complex cant be attained
So amazing so adorable
So appealing from the view
The one l choice.
Cant wait to see her finally
En my life just forever mine
No other girl a part from her
Ready to spend pesos y dinero
Each day de mi la novia
Surely heart has settled
For first time in decades
Sophie has made surprise
To me cant wait to see
The enthusiastic life
Juntos con mi amigos
The one I choice.

Composed by Tibez Albershile

133.What after break up

"What after break up"
Tell me ready to hear
The sweetness sounds
Still loading on mi mind
Thought gonna be gone
By esta reloj indeed it's
Complex cutting story
So toxic love story
What after break up
Maybe cry down cheek
Losing love yet being loyal
However life give us lifetime
True partners, true love
Stii optimistic as only option
I gonna get from jah
Can't give up still firm
Kicking keenly keeping
Over view on next step
What after break up
Love trust and all care
Gone where the other
Secondary need go
It's time to seek secular
Peace con my padre
My mentor rest are just
Worldly things which can
Be changed just con
Time indeed time its
Everything can't imagine
Can't believe

What after break up.
Nothing awesome like
Self realising toward right
Path leaving last stories
Indeed it's awesome
She flew for real but
After lighting little light
Can't find a way a method
Just to say thank you
Some leaves , for best
To allow transformation
To allow change charge
For best for anos
Composed by Tibez Albershile

134. Shake me

"Shake me"
Shake me the soul
Sophie is gonna go
Tell me she isn't anyone
Your favourito is gone
Find another one no
One knows nor thought
Yet we are optimistic
Shake me shake me.
Heart to heart
Love of eternity
Love of giving call love
De mi life so amazing
Sophie so simple
Even l feel to play
Little of hide and seek
Shake me of flewing away
Shake me shake me .
I got her and her alone
Got back good but now
I just got Sophie so lovely
To spend moments together
Indeed is memorial scene
Even sky can bear witness
Cant risk nor thought
To shake her just to shake
Her hands and heart alone
Shake me shake me.
The fear of fellows
Good in games

Cant even think l got
Her alone can't imagine
Day without her just
Me and her like mother
With children can't
Think nor imagine
The minutes more
Close to her and her
Shake me shake me.
Composed by Tibez Albershile

135.Farewell

" Farewell"
Indeed it's a byee byee
From years to months
Months to weeks so
Sad to see it's minutes
Tears down the cheek
Indeed it's a farewell.
So sad to say
It to see enthusiastic
Leadership down
Brothers and sisters
It's a sad farewell
Who knows nor
Thought of indeed
It's a climax
Just memories
Of best moments
Down the line
Indeed it's farewell .
God always has
Best plans for
All and the entire
Society and socialization
In our mmuca has
Indeed impacted
To us for best mmuca
Community en future
Adiós bro , adiós sister
Indeed it's a farewell.
What can we say

If not success
To your next journey
That is full of ups and downs
Yet your optimistic we
Are Sure nothing granite
A head of you
Adiós brother, adiós sister
Indeed it's a farewell.
Composed by Tibez Albershile

136.Justice

"Justice"
We wanna justice, for all,
All put down five, fit the ground,
One died following , the rule of law,
What we want , is only justice.,
No man is above the law, that what we know,
If no justice tell, Kenya to know,
No justice for, children died,
Imagine the 12 years old, death,
By gun bullet, yet family can not ,
Get justice , yet we have law !,
What is the work , of 18 billion ?,
Let Kenyan to know, the use of the money.,
Day time killing , just in the name of police,
Do we have law , maybe we have raw ,
So sorry to , brother y sister .,
Imagine the pain for mother, who receives no justice.,
Created by Alberto Kelly

137. Cual dai

"Cual dai"
Am a statue on mi
Satution what to say
So complex cero
Pesos y dinero
Cual dai no Migos
Kelly gonna ask
Ayuda am statue
My state Migos
Es wanting what
I gonna do esta
Life l didn't see
Even un poco light
Cual dai
No call no one
Paying heed to
Cual dai only
Preguntas mi personas
Se sientes a domir
But no comida even
Un poco domir es granite
Just molecules de agua
I wonder wiii l see nuevo
Day day to fulfill mi dreams
Cual dai
Life sweet con
Pesos o dinero
Hoy yo see mi self
As example en earth
De personas de cero

Pesos y dinero
No comida left de Kelly
Even no Skylark de Kelly
Yo gonna hablamous a
Cual dai
When everything es
So difficult even
Tears cheek can't
Make it right
Stiii optimistic of
Better tomorrow
Miles Kelly l have gone
Still going despite
How matters at hand
Cual dai
Composed by Tibez Albershile

138.Where were you

"Where were you"
Where were you
When l was mocked
Where were you when
I went behind bars
When did you turn
To murderer when
Where were you
When everyone
Evacuated from myself
When l was seen as criminal
When l was almost dead
Where were you
Just tell me l wanna
Here when did lover
Turned to murderer
When how why tell me
Where were you
When everything l worked
Hard turning to ashes
Where were you
When even my parents were
Being harassed harmed
Psychological and physical
Where were you tell me
Time we spent together
I see l found an angel
But now am devil itself
Can't believe cant say
Where did you hide to

When l was denied my
Rights as citizen just
For you where were you
When all this happened
I wanna answers
Yet fate can't be changed
You are chameleon indeed
Where were you where were you
Composed by Tibez Albershile

139.La novia

"La novia"
I have actually found my first and true love
I wonder what gift l gonna give her
His pretty has put me the sky l am amazed
Just looking at her simple eyes l feel eternal bond
She has actually secured my heart
I never thought of anybody else apart from her
Many are trying but am lost at his love
My bodyand soul am giving her as a gift my love
What make me happy is knowing of how loyal to me and our father
Her name joan has made me to start a love journal with her
My simplicity lifestyle has actually found a teacher for that section
I can't shy shouting to universe the way she loves me
No matter how complex satution is l gonna love her as my only love
For sure this life l have found a heart
Where l gonna rest no more reckless life now
I wish to sing a love song for my Amor
Composed by Alberto Kelly

140Pregunta

"Pregunta"
Age to age refer me
They tease me what
I gonna do or get now
Encanta end of my time
Is coming as lighting
To who to seek advice
What wiii be tomorrow
I found Encanta interesting
But now to tears
Cant believe nor
Say to people see
Me in such state
From mi previous fantastic
Encanta life but hoy
Melodies stucking
Soon am growing ripe
To whom should l
Seek just little step
De Encanta am statue
To l referred to rightful
Partners have moved
Long time when l lost
En esta life so where
Should l go to seek
Encanta who gonna
Elaborate to me
Who to eradicate
Mi dilemma of mine
Tibez yet time

Miles to go juntos
As l didn't expect
Yet mistry to me
Didn't be see value
De Encanta de Joan
Just see joking machine
Even wise turn worst
From making decisions
Worst error l ever experience
Only Jah can join me
Back before memories
Erase me en esta journey
Composed by Tibez Albershile

141.lust

"lust"
Where when did it started,
My mind and soul one thing,
How to face the dilemma now,
What to do now,
No one to ask advice now,
Tell me how to manage now,
My lifetime l haven't thought of tiii now,
Call me now
Am tired can l separate,
My body and mind now,
This life am completely tied,
The state and stage l don't,
Know best solution out now,
Call me shy to next stage,
I thought day without this yet,
Now l am captive continues,
I laughed last my friends,
Yet hoy it's me more sad,
Whom wiii erase this evil,
Am ready to do anything ,
I can't share l can't see myself,
In much pain more continues,
Day in out dreams world,
Am starting to slowly going,
To it for real am completely,
Afraid better to agree with,
My father in prayers than domir,
To see imaginary images you ,
Even dont expect to see in life,

Composed by Tibez Albershile

142.Thoughts

"Thoughts"
Actually am working ,with enemies everywhere,
I can't believe, what l saw l thought l was in deep sleep,
But that was the reality, not a dream day in and out,
My friends had informed me ,but l was so dedicated daily to her,
I feel like standing, in deep sea so as to be swept away by sea current,
Am lost completely in, deep sea of questions without answers,
Was l wasting ,my precious time talking to you ,
I had given you my heart, but but you hurted my feelings fearlessly,
Seeing your status, l felt like nature was sending message to me,
I made a mistake of choosing you over one girl whom loved me
sincerely simplicity was her style,
I thought of such my eyes, are full of tears tirelessly,
Why after all the people, whom l know you, mi Amor
So painful story , even l fear to say ,
The way l was so boastful, of love,
Yet today l am lying, alone let me,
Remain calm , as dead now l can't,
Add value to you, am no longer lover,
Amazing things we did, contigo gonna go,
Only preguntas in mind, the juntas tiii eternity is where,
World is full of wild beasts, who hide in the name of love,
When all occurred , when my stories turned toxic,
No more of Skylark , amor even sunshine all lost as berbel ,
Only mi padre ,can entail when tables turned,
Chameleon nature cant be predict, yet we call ourselves humans,
Composed by Tibez Albershile

143 Teacher

"Teacher"
Surely whom gonna be like a teacher in this state,
Teacher are pillars ,of our personalities with start from our mothers,
Whom are our first, Closely friends and teachers,
Who gives us identity, in our society for socialization,
Moving further we have many teachers, whom if we start to say end of time wiii be climax,
Without forgetting that we are teachers, to our lives in various ways ,
Who can be like teacher, sleepless nights to see you sons and daughters successful,
In life while you are mocking day in out as their silent nature ,leave the remaining to almighty,
It's high time to impress the spirit of supporting teacher hood culture, in our society so to stay peaceful,
Life of our children's are on our hands, either we spoil or take them to right path,
By molding them with virtues, through education and daily life experiences,
So we can have a great society, that has been aim of teachers,
Regardless ,of various response from various people,
We are teachers and we will continue being teachers ,
We have come from grass ,to graze lets transform our society ,
with our knowledge, as key for eradication of stupidity,
Let's stand firm ,as affirmative to support this teacher hood culture,
Together indeed , we can no one is limited,
We are family forever, for the best of our future ,
Time has best remedy, we gonna work juntos just to see success,
Composed by Alberto Kelly
Country Kenya ⟡⟡ ⟡⟡ ⟡⟡

144.Sweet love

"Sweet love '
Your small heart l have found a place to hide
Your simplicity has signified me to change my marital status of single
Your beauty has brought blight to my life
Your sex eyes have made me sin just seeing you
Your sweet sound has turned out to be my santuri
Your love has completed me my companion
Your album of pictures has acted as shield against seek cheek
Your love has made me to lost in your heart
Your pretty has purified me to be holy without no sin
Your forgiveness has made our relationship to rust forever
Your message has molded me to be better person
Your unconditionally love has inspired me to improve and love you
day in and out
Your honest has brought honor in honorable places
Your sweetness has swim into my life giving me identity
Your love surely is meant to stay
I don't think l can give my heart to anyone anywhere apart from you
sweetheart
You give me definition of love Liz
I don't think there is love without you my love
Created by Albert Nyangaresi

145.mi pet

"Mi favorito"
What l gonna say
Your beauty has
Let me to stare
Each day l feel
To feed you forever
You are mine and mine
I don't need any other
Day en out donkey
You make me feel
To sing a lala bay
What l fear is
Seeing someone
Taking you away
You are mi world
Your duties are great
What to say to them
They say am en love
Con you mi pet
Let them hablamous
Anything but your
Position es next
To mi heart how
Great having guard
En your heart it's honor
Pet en human heart
What name l gonna
Call you mi pet
Can't see you as donkey
I see as mi universe

That created de me
Ready to go miles
Con you mi universe

Composed by Tibez Albershile

146. Eternity Rest

"Eternity Rest"
Sir Jah , we grant our legends,
We give you our, heroes to you,
Our request , to you Sir Jah ,
Allow them to have , eternal rest,
They fought , a freedom fight.,
Your brother's , y sister celebrates,
Your victory , your voice for this nation,
Your voice it's recognised, en earth,
We wanna Gen Z , heroes to rest en peace,
We trust , almighty gonna grant justice,
Justice for your souls, no justice en esta nation,
He gonna judge all , regardless their earthly powers y position,
We wanna your souls, to rest tiii meet again .,
Adiós sister , adiós brother,
No one planned this, nor expected ,
Adiós my son y my daughter tiii we meet,
When you are called , you have responded very well .,
Composed by Alberto Kelly

147.Kizito Family

"The Kizito family"
Sure Kizito is kicking in academic
Each day each individual is trying to come success in education
To excel in education there are many programs put in place
Since success is a communal work consideration of individualism
Student are sacrificing their midnight making their future brighter
The principal is busy putting in resources for his children to excel in
education
Day in out teacher are teaching committedly to see their children pass
exam and be men in society
The school it is self has conducive environment for conducting studies
The workers are working days and night to see that the program in
place are running
The co -culucular activities are making the body be strong and healthy
for studies
In terms of nutrition Kizito is known of quality not of quantity
Finally family is always United likewise to Kizito is one one various
levels
Composed by Albert Nyangaresi

148. Mmarau

"Mmarau"
We have actually, arrived home far from home,
Where many we have been, waiting for,
A home to write our academic, stories from start to end,
We believe in spirit, our dreams day in out wiii be fulfilled,
The warm welcome,we have received as mother and child,
We feel to shout to universe, to see the love of our lectures,
The are eagerly to impact knowledge, to us to be key to society in
various forms,
The program in place, are so inspiring to see success,
Like other institutions also, mmarau has motto that inspires alot,
When one is going astray, the motto act as his mentor,
A part from programs,the institution has avail internet,
For online learning and encourage learner, to do more on field of
research,
The library also is available for those ready to explore,more in various
fields for success,
The environment is so touching, to allow one to take studies peaceful ,
The security is on day and night to assure student are secure to fulfil
their dreams,
The security department ,also ensure off-campus security for good
mentality and focus in academic,
Surely we can't say, that there is a good institution like mmarau in
academic success,
And the institution believe, that with grace of God all impossible is
possible,
Making Maasai Mara university God fearing institution,
Sky might be limit, success is assured in mmarau,
Composed by© Tiberius Alberto

149. Valentino

"Valentino "
Valentine's day,
The day of love,
The day of white feathered doves,
The day we express our true inner feelings,
To the one in heart,
The day I met you,
I would never rue,
The day our eyes met,
And the burning sensation of newly found love,
Glimmered in our hearts,
The most beautiful thing of a young love,
The truth that came with it,
I found Favor in your love,
A true one from above,
Day l found freedom freely,
With my Amor playing hide,
Seek game starting from,
Sunrise to sunset ,
What l gonna tell my valentine,
My favourito one whom l,
Love so much , let universe give,
Me some small piece to impress,
My valentine mi Amor ,
This day l gonna see mountain,
Valley in valentine nothing,
Is impossible mi little angel,
Sing santuri for me ,
Call all names you feel to fed,
Me my love little by little flow,

Of love tiii climax of deed day,
Composed by Janet ft Tibez

150.Sunshine

"Sunshine"
I wanna feel feelings,
Mi amor don't fail me,
I wanna taste at least,
First time for while ,
I hear love y read poems,
Yet l don't know love ,
Can't you feed me ,
I really wanna love,
Am tired of games dear,
Days in out l feel,
So lonely dear can't,
You even liar to me,
With hag beb,
I can't really remember,
When l received love,
Maybe my mother love,
Mi world why don't you,
Give me even little laugh,
With love my lovely,
Heart whom l have chosen,
Over millions mi Moonlight,
Don't you see how much l ,
Really care for you,
Can a dai go down,
Without seeing you,
Album mi Amor
I can't imagine life
Without my love my darling,
I better freeze to a statue ,

Leaving mi Amor is granite,
In my life l really Encanta estas,
Mucho mi heart ,
I wanna know love ,
From mi Amor,
They say am freeze,
I don't have love mi,
Amor l really wanna,
Listen to your love,
Knowledge to my key,
Of my life my bird l ,
Wiii be your learner con ,
Esta world mi Amor,
Composed by Tibez Albershile

151.kicd

"What A Greatful kicd"
Time has changed , indeed this new error,
The error of creativity and innovation ,
Thanks to good governance and co operation with kicd,
We are able to see better tomorrow,
Better generation that's is through cbc,
Indeed we are Greatful to kicd.
The teacher played their role ,
To come up with this program,
The program that see that ,
All learns aren't the same as we see,
They need a program that fit them ,
The learners have talents, abilities ,
To do great things however the abilities
Are buried five fit ground thanks to ,
The kicd tomorrow is shining from far,
Indeed we are grateful to kicd.
The creative learners such as poets
Such as story creators are identified
In earliest stages and the building
For them starts from the moment
The school supplies the relevant
Material that are provided by kicd
The creativity of learners progress
Keep moving to higher levels
Indeed we are greatful to kicd.
The new program indeed its best ,
For what it offers we are assured ,
Of great future and generations,
The role of creative arts, and sports arts,

Play another part to our children cant ,
Imagine of the program for people ,
Of this republic children ,
Can't hide our gratitude to KICD,
For this and any other coming ,
Indeed we are greatfu to kicd.
No man on his own island
We need support from each other
We need co operation from parents
To stake holders not school alone
But home
Teacher play their role in school
Parents and community also
Need to play the role to see better
Nation tomorrow kicd has done
The best we deeply need to say
Even once thanks to management
Indeed we are greatfu to Kicd.
The program also does acknowledge
That the connection and the bond,
That co exist between the imaginative,
Without leaving behind the subjects ,
Together with the basic skills ,
In manner the program further more,
On the practical parts compared to
The theoretical part unlike the previous,
Thanks for well job done by kicd
Indeed we are greatfu to kicd.

For real education is the real treasure,
The creativity and imagination ,

Gonna build a innovative and inventive,
Generation and that was the central idea,
Central aim to have our own ,
From creativity nation can grow and develop
This as come from the help of kicd
Indeed we are greatfu to kicd.
The nation hasn't been left behind ,
Too it has come up with the organisation ,
Such a as kmf that see the special ,
Gifts or talents and build the talents,
This hasn't been so simple as a b c ,
All has been done by co operation ,
Co ordination both kicd and Government ,
Thus the program the learners are enjoying ,
Their recognition by kicd
What amazing department for education,
kicd for better tomorrow,
Indeed we are greatfu to kicd.
Composed by Alberto Kelly

152. Jubilee life insurance

"jubilee life insurance "
Life is a gift and gift its treasured,
A home where you gonna get all,
Your support help it's here in our,
Jubilee life insurance miles come,
Tii to date people are losing lifes,
Today you have chance to change,
To best take a step end poverty ,
Children are getting educated,
The one having investment here is home,
Don't fear jubilee life insurance is home,
What amazing its jubilee.
The aim our jubilee isn't money,
Many wanna think money yet,
We value life and living status,
We are here to help to pace ,
A good society so admirable by ,
The coming generations it's jubilee ,
Life insurance that gonna solve so ,
Complex state of your life values,
Integrity , loyalty and honesty are valued,
Society it's made of values and value,
Is the community and jubilee it's home,
For years to come years to go ,
What amazing its jubilee.
No man on his own island we journey,
With you just as mother and children ,
We can't forget you in good and bad,
Times we stand firm affirmative to see,
Our client at peace so don't allow,

Chance at hand to flew away just ,
Use the opportunity at hand and ask ,
The procedure to be present on the list,
What amazing its jubilee.
Here it's a place to stay by view,
We give financial solutions so ,
Grab chance today no one ,
Knows tomorrow today the,
Available opportunity might ,
Be not available things change,
Dynamic but change for best,
The solutions are forever in ,
Your life to reduce burden ,
It's jubilee journey we jion ,
Free from stress to clients,
All the pain is sorted out,
What amazing its jubilee.
Worry less we handle even aged,
Those retired it's matter to invest,
When retirement period reach you,
Just stiii enjoy your life by jubilee insurance life you invited,
It's here to stay start today next day,
Invite friends to join for this is best,
Not for individual but society,
Chase peace not pieces it's jubilee life insurance best and stil best ,
What amazing its jubilee.

What amazing project platform,
Organisation it's jubilee life insurance ,
Our lives and our beloved ones are save,
Our wealth transfer it's done at ease,

We enjoy the tax relief it's jubilee,
The sweetness of jubilee insurance,
Leave me to stare many offers to see,
People at peace so grateful let's ,
Follow up simple process for better tomorrow,
Jubilee life insurance is here today,
Jubilee is here tomorrow also generation,
Coming
What amazing its jubilee.
Composed by Tibez Albershile

153. Counterfeit

"counterfeit"
Nothing comes just on bear hands,
We think short cuts are key to success,
We are completely wrong believe me,
We are actually lowering our standards,
When wiii we style up each day same,
Topic same story it's counterfeit again,
counterfeit counterfeit.
We are crying to seek support,
What support we need actually,
Am worried when we leave legit,
Commodities to seek similar goods,
So sorry to see we are not careful ,
With our choice of commodities,
Cosmetic , alcohol , foods staffs
Cheap in nature yet chaos to life,
We are lighting to chase them chasing,
Illness to our bodies ,
counterfeit counterfeit.
We are counting days down line,
Our healthcare services are at risk ,
We are ignoring good services for ,
Fraud and fake results ,
Cant believe we are killing ourselves,
Forgetting cheap is expensive tears,
Down cheek yet you cant realize,
counterfeit is taking Life counterfeit,
Who gonna erase it counterfeit,
counterfeit counterfeit.
We are busy creating jobs just ,

Like jokes you are destroying jobs,
We are losing quality we gain quantities,
What agony where are we moving ,
Worries we are chasing legit good s,
Just for copyright good cant imagine,
counterfeit it's attacking everything,
Not one sector but all,
counterfeit counterfeit,
Youths are just utilize the youth ,
In social platforms like YouTube,
To create new creations to sad,
To hear the content is already ,
In market innovation and creativity,
It's facing worst face just as results,
counterfeit where to seek help ,
Who to seek refugee,
counterfeit counterfeit .
Gorvement is going on worst face,
Just as no tax no tax of good,
Good are entering market more,
However no more information ,
The source and channel just,
That brought to market no tax ,
Yet call for help to our roads,
Our education where money ,
Gonna come from no tax,
counterfeit counterfeit .
We are ready to build best ,
House to stay but our nature,
To obtain materials to our mansion,
Is from same source counterfeit,
We are ready to chase poor goods,

Without considering our lives,
Gonna go down to soil,
Just by our reckless just lets style up,
Woke up our lives are at stake,
counterfeit is finishing us so ,
Let's chase change before changes ,
Have changed us ,
counterfeit counterfeit.
Composed by Tibez Albershile

154. TB

"TB"
What agony where ,
Did this disease arose,
Do you know it it's TB,
The airborne disease ,
Day in out doctors ,
Are busy try to seek,
Cure yet no cure ,
Is there it's as result,
Of smoking so be careful,
It affects the lungs ,
However other parts can,
Be at risk right from brains,
TB
"TB"

The disease is killing,
Don't waste opportunity ,
Open up share status ,
When you see weight loss,
See fever also night sweats,
Why to waste opportunity,
Seek medical at earliest ,
Indeed no cure when it's
On the final stages starting,
Of the TB believe me you,
Gonna recover and be firm,
TB TB .

Life is precious so ,
Be your brothers keeper,
TB is killing don't shy ,
Community come on,
Be simple as a,b,c you,
Can get help stigmatization,
I can see if damaging us ,
Yet we are same people ,
Wasting our time not ,
Sharing yet we share ,
Things of less value,
Sure let's be so careful,
TB TB .
No age is safe ,
Not rich nor poor,
Everyone is at risk,
Dead knows no body,
Seek medication ,
Make doctors day in,
Day out your darling ,
See how your health ,
Gonna prosper seek,
Medication seek advice,
TB is here to stay ,
Stay safe stay building,
The nations and generations.
Composed by Tibez Albershile

155. Political

Political
Where are they ,with their promises,
I am worried, my mind is not calm at all,
I am helpless seeing ,what is the satution today,
Their false promises ,make me fail to understand,
What and when ,people see the reality,
When wiii people vote ,wisely for leaders,
Corruption is dominating, continues as disease,
Yet we all have better, solution for satution.
When , whom gonna put the corrupted official behind bars,
What surprise me ,is when the court is leading ,
Cases are sent, but since of poverty you lose for the high class,
Where wiii we get justice ,for sure so shameful,
Current condition, is calling for help from outside ,
I am witnessing, without anything to say to comment,
The living standard is high, yet high class can't see ,
They are ready to snatch ,everything even a single cent,
So sorry to see such ,painful ruling in the republic.
Where are we going to hide ,our eyes from seeing ,
The evils that is conducted by this current class of ruler's,
Am worried why ,did we waste our vote to vote ,
Where is the work ,to us when you are qualified yet you are denied
while some from their ascent is given,
When wiii we mature, we leave tribalism as culture we progress
particularly ,
What is the meaning, of education if it ends up to nothing ,
So painful to say, that you are in an independent nation while full of
natives.
Composed by Albert Nyangaresi

The

The